ASIA BOND MONITOR
MARCH 2023

ASIAN DEVELOPMENT BANK

ADB

Contents

Emerging East Asian Local Currency Bond Markets: A Regional Update

Emerging East Asian Local Currency Bond Markets: A Regional Update

Executive Summary

Recent Developments in Financial Conditions in Emerging East Asia

Financial conditions in emerging East Asian economies improved modestly but were clouded by heightened uncertainty in the trajectory of United States (US) monetary policy tightening during the review period of 30 November to 10 March.[1] In December 2022 and January 2023, financial conditions in the region recovered strongly as bond yields declined, equity markets gained, risk premiums narrowed, and currencies strengthened across most regional markets. The improvement was largely driven by the easing of recession risk; the moderating pace of monetary tightening by the US Federal Reserve; and downward trending inflation in the US, euro area, and many regional economies. However, from 1 February through 10 March, regional financial conditions weakened over rising uncertainty regarding the pace of the Federal Reserve's monetary tightening and market turmoil due to the collapse of Silicon Valley Bank and Signature Bank, and, subsequently, pressure on Credit Suisse that led to its takeover.

From 30 November to 10 March, emerging East Asian currencies strengthened by a gross domestic product (GDP)-weighted average of 2.1% against the US dollar. Most of this strengthening occurred in December 2022–January 2023 when the region's currencies gained a GDP-weighted average of 5.0%. This was in contrast with a 2.7% depreciation against the US dollar from 1 February to 10 March. Credit default swap spreads, a proxy for risk premiums, posted a GDP-weighted narrowing of 3 basis points (bps) during the overall review period. However, a collective widening of risk premiums was seen from 1 February through 10 March.

Emerging East Asian equity markets gained a market-value-weighted return of 1.6% during the review period, driven by market rallies in the People's Republic of China (PRC) and Hong Kong, China on the PRC's reopening.

Excluding the PRC and Hong Kong, China, the region's markets recorded a value-weighted loss of 3.1% during the review period. Similar to regional currencies, emerging East Asian markets collectively gained during December 2022–January 2023, which saw a value-weighted return of 5.7%, contrasting with a loss of 3.6% from 1 February to 10 March.

Yields on 2-year and 10-year local currency (LCY) government bonds trended down in most emerging East Asian markets during the review period, posting a simple average decline of 12 bps and 18 bps, respectively. The region's 2-year and 10-year yields fell an average of 35 bps and 36 bps, respectively, in December 2022–January 2023, before rising 23 bps and 18 bps, respectively, from 1 February to 10 March.

Portfolio inflows were observed in regional capital markets during the review period. From 30 November to 10 March, the region received net foreign equity inflows of USD31.9 billion. The majority of these inflows were attributed to the PRC on optimism over its economic reopening. In December 2022–January 2023, the region's bond markets recorded net foreign bond inflows amounting to USD1.7 billion.

Risks to regional financial conditions remain tilted to the downside. Key risks include uncertainty in the path of the Federal Reserve's monetary tightening, the persistence of elevated inflation, and uncertainties in the economic outlooks of major advanced and regional economies. High asset prices and rising debt levels generated during the low-interest-rate era may result in vulnerabilities in the balance sheets of some financial institutions and corporates. Liquidity stress has been experienced by real estate companies in the Viet Nam corporate bond market as they find it hard to refinance their debt. The recent turmoil in the US and European banking sectors highlights the importance of liquidity buffers and proper risk management amid tightened financial conditions and the dimmed economic outlook.

---

[1] Emerging East Asia is defined to include member states of the Association of Southeast Asian Nations (ASEAN) plus the People's Republic of China; Hong Kong, China; and the Republic of Korea.

Recent Developments in Local Currency Bond Markets in Emerging East Asia

LCY bonds outstanding in emerging East Asian markets stood at USD23.2 trillion at the end of December. Growth in the LCY bond market moderated to 1.2% quarter-on-quarter (q-o-q) in the fourth quarter (Q4) of 2022 from 2.3% q-o-q in the previous quarter as regional issuance contracted. Government bonds accounted for 63.9% of the outstanding bond stock in emerging East Asia at the end of December, with a total amount of USD14.8 trillion. Growth in the government bond market eased to 1.9% q-o-q in Q4 2022 from 2.8% q-o-q in the previous quarter. Meanwhile, corporate bonds outstanding contracted 0.1% q-o-q to fall to USD8.4 trillion at the end of December. The aggregate LCY bond stock of Association of Southeast Asian Nations (ASEAN) member economies reached USD2.1 trillion at the end of December, comprising 8.9% of the region's total LCY bond market.

In Q4 2022, regional LCY bond issuance contracted 6.7% compared with the previous quarter to USD2.2 trillion. Both the government and corporate bond segments witnessed contractions in Q4 2022, as most governments had fulfilled the majority of their borrowing requirements in earlier quarters and rising borrowing costs curtailed bond issuance among corporates. LCY bond issuance in ASEAN markets totaled USD456.4 billion, accounting for 20.9% of the regional issuance total during the quarter. On a year-on-year (y-o-y) basis, regional issuance declined 1.9% in Q4 2022, dragged down by a 15.0% contraction in the corporate bond segment. However, full-year issuance volume reached a record-high of USD9.0 trillion in 2022, up 6.8% y-o-y from USD8.4 trillion in 2021.

More than half of emerging East Asia's government bonds outstanding and bond issuance in Q4 2022 comprised medium- to longer-term maturities. At the end of December, 54.4% of the region's outstanding government bonds carried tenors of 5 years or longer, and the size-weighted tenor of outstanding LCY government bonds in emerging East Asia was 9.1 years. The size-weighted tenor of LCY government bond issuance in Q4 2022 was 5.9 years, with 60.4% of government bond issuances in Q4 2022 having tenors of 5 years or longer. The majority of LCY government bonds outstanding continued to be held by banks, insurance companies, and pension funds at the end of December.

Sustainable bonds outstanding in ASEAN+3 reached USD589.3 billion at the end of December.[2] Growth in the regional sustainable bond market moderated to 36.7% y-o-y in 2022 from 53.8% y-o-y in 2021, but this was still faster than the global market's growth of 27.2% in 2022. Compared with the overall bond market, ASEAN+3 sustainable bonds accounted for only 1.7% of ASEAN+3's aggregate bonds outstanding at the end of December. The ASEAN+3 sustainable bond market is dominated by LCY financing (64.7%) and private sector financing (77.8%). Around 54% of outstanding sustainable bonds at the end of December carried a remaining maturity of less than 3 years. In terms of issuance, 78.9% of regional sustainable bonds issued in 2022 carried maturities of 5 years or less, 76.8% came from the private sector, and 72.6% were issued in domestic currencies.

AsianBondsOnline 2022 Bond Market Liquidity Survey

Emerging East Asia's LCY bond market saw an overall weakening of liquidity conditions in 2022 compared with 2021. This was largely driven by tightened financial conditions in both global and domestic financial markets. About 61% of respondents to the *AsianBondsOnline* 2022 Bond Market Liquidity Survey noted that overall liquidity declined, bid–ask spreads widened, and transaction sizes narrowed in both government and corporate bond markets across the region. Participants cited domestic and US monetary policy tightening as the top two factors contributing to weakened liquidity conditions in 2022. The survey's findings also indicated that liquidity conditions in conventional bond markets and sustainable bond markets were largely comparable. Among structural issues, the availability of hedging instruments remained the least-developed aspect of the market that requires further policy initiatives for development.

---

[2] ASEAN+3 is defined to include member states of the Association of Southeast Asian Nations (ASEAN) plus the People's Republic of China; Hong Kong, China; Japan; and the Republic of Korea.

Global and Regional Market Developments

Improved financial conditions in emerging East Asia are clouded by uncertainty over the path of monetary tightening in the United States.

Financial conditions in most emerging East Asian economies modestly improved during the review period from 30 November 2022 to 10 March 2023.[1] In December 2022 and January 2023, regional financial conditions collectively improved largely on the expected moderation of monetary tightening in major advanced economies as well as the peaking of domestic inflation in many regional economies. Risk premiums narrowed, equity markets gained, currencies strengthened against the United States (US) dollar, and bond yields fell between 30 November 2022 and 31 January 2023. However, heightened uncertainties regarding the Federal Reserve's monetary path and market turmoil associated with the collapse of Silicon Valley Bank cast a cloud over regional financial conditions in February and early March, especially in equity markets. Market concerns were then exacerbated by concerns over Credit Suisse in Europe that eventually led to its being taken over by UBS. Most long-term bond yields fell in the region during the review period, while net portfolio investment inflows were observed in many regional capital markets (**Table A**).

In major advanced economies, bond yields continued to rise as their central banks sustained monetary tightening and inflation remained elevated (**Table B**). In the US and Germany, short-term bond yields, which track policy rates closely, rose more than long-term bond yields, which tend to price in inflationary factors. In Japan, where policy rates remained unchanged during the review period, the 2-year government bond yield barely moved, and the 10-year bond yield rose on rising inflation and speculation that the Bank of Japan (BOJ) would pivot from its current monetary policy stance.

Table A: Changes in Financial Conditions in Major Advanced Economies and Select Emerging East Asian Markets (Between 30 November 2022 and 10 March 2023)

	2-Year Government Bond (bps)	10-Year Government Bond (bps)	5-Year Credit Default Swap Spread (bps)	Equity Index (%)	FX Rate (%)
Major Advanced Economies					
United States	28	9	–	(5.4)	–
United Kingdom	35	48	(4)	2.3	(0.2)
Japan	(0.1)	16	0.8	1.6	2.3
Germany	97	58	(5)	7.2	2.3
Select Emerging East Asian Markets					
China, People's Rep. of	7	(4)	(3)	2.5	2.5
Hong Kong, China	(53)	18	–	3.9	(0.5)
Indonesia	24	2	9	(4.5)	1.8
Korea, Rep. of	(9)	(10)	(7)	(3.2)	(0.5)
Malaysia	(24)	(16)	0.1	(3.7)	(1.7)
Philippines	(11)	(86)	7	(2.8)	2.6
Singapore	41	16	–	(3.4)	0.8
Thailand	6	(21)	(11)	(2.2)	0.6
Viet Nam	(94)	(60)	(11)	0.4	4.3

( ) = negative, – = not available, bps = basis points, FX = foreign exchange.
Note: A positive (negative) value for the FX rate indicates the appreciation (depreciation) of the local currency against the United States dollar.
Source: *AsianBondsOnline* computations based on Bloomberg LP data.

---

[1] Emerging East Asia is defined to include member states of the Association of Southeast Asian Nations (ASEAN) plus the People's Republic of China; Hong Kong, China; and the Republic of Korea.

Table B: Changes in Monetary Stances in Major Advanced Economies and Select Emerging East Asian Markets

Economy	Policy Rate 1-Mar-2022 (%)	Rate Change (%)													Policy Rate 10-Mar-2023 (%)	Change in Policy Rates (basis points)
		Mar-2022	Apr-2022	May-2022	Jun-2022	Jul-2022	Aug-2022	Sep-2022	Oct-2022	Nov-2022	Dec-2022	Jan-2023	Feb-2023	Mar-2023		
United States	0.25	↑0.25		↑0.50	↑0.75	↑0.75		↑0.75		↑0.75	↑0.50		↑0.25		4.75	↑450
Euro Area	(0.50)					↑0.50		↑0.75		↑0.75	↑0.50		↑0.50		2.50	↑300
United Kingdom	0.50	↑0.25		↑0.25	↑0.25		↑0.50	↑0.50		↑0.75	↑0.50		↑0.50		4.00	↑350
Japan	(0.10)														(0.10)	
China, People's Rep. of	2.85						↓0.10								2.75	↓ 10
Indonesia	3.50						↑0.25	↑0.50	↑0.50	↑0.50	↑0.25	↑0.25			5.75	↑225
Korea, Rep. of	1.25		↑0.25	↑0.25		↑0.50	↑0.25		↑0.50	↑0.25		↑0.25			3.50	↑225
Malaysia	1.75			↑0.25		↑0.25		↑0.25		↑0.25					2.75	↑100
Philippines	2.00			↑0.25	↑0.25	↑0.75	↑0.50	↑0.50		↑0.75	↑0.50		↑0.50		6.00	↑400
Singapore	–		↑			↑			↑						–	–
Thailand	0.50						↑0.25	↑0.25		↑0.25		↑0.25			1.50	↑100
Viet Nam	4.00							↑1.00	↑1.00						6.00	↑200

( ) = negative.

Notes:
1. Data coverage is from 1 March 2022 to 10 March 2023.
2. For the People's Republic of China, data used in the chart are for the 1-year medium-term lending facility rate. While the 1-year benchmark lending rate is the official policy rate of the People's Bank of China, market players use the 1-year medium-term lending facility rate as a guide for the monetary policy direction of the People's Bank of China.
3. The up (down) arrow for Singapore signifies monetary policy tightening (loosening) by its central bank. The Monetary Authority of Singapore utilizes the Singapore dollar nominal effective exchange rate (S$NEER) to guide its monetary policy.

Sources: Various central bank websites.

The expected pace of US monetary tightening shifted during the review period. In December 2022 and January 2023, a moderation in monetary tightening was expected on softening inflation in the US, where year-on-year (y-o-y) consumer price inflation continued trending downward from June's 9.1% peak to 7.7%, 7.1%, and 6.5% in October, November, and December, respectively. Personal Consumption Expenditures (PCE) inflation also declined from 6.3% y-o-y in September to y-o-y readings of 6.1%, 5.6%, and 5.3% for October, November, and December, respectively. During the 13–14 December Federal Open Market Committee (FOMC) meeting, the Federal Reserve narrowed the policy rate hike to 50 basis points (bps) after hikes of 75 bps each in its past four meetings.

Uncertainties regarding the future direction of the Federal Reserve's monetary policy heightened in February and early March. Although the Federal Reserve hiked the policy rate by 25 bps, as expected, during the 31 January–1 February FOMC meeting, chances of a 50 bps rate hike at the March FOMC meeting increased from zero on 3 February to 24% on 28 February. In February, the Federal Reserve stated that inflation remained elevated with no sign of quickly falling.[2] Although consumer price inflation in the US further declined to 6.4% y-o-y in January and 6.0% y-o-y in February—from 6.5% y-o-y in December—core inflation remained persistent. PCE inflation also rose slightly in January to 5.4% y-o-y from 5.3% y-o-y in December. The 22 February release of minutes from the 31 January–1 February FOMC meeting indicated that members still found inflation "unacceptably high" and they continued to worry about inflation. The minutes also indicated that some participants were in favor of a 50 bps rate hike as opposed to the eventual 25 bps rate hike. The collapse of Silicon Valley Bank further clouded the market with uncertainty over the Federal Reserve's monetary policy path. Per the CME FedWatch, the likelihood of a 50 bps rate hike abated as investors believed the Federal Reserve may become cautious to minimize volatility that could lead to bank failures similar to that of Silicon Valley Bank. The probability of a 50 bps rate hike fell to zero on 13 March from 40.2% the previous day.

Market expectations were borne out when the Federal Reserve raised the federal funds target range by 25 bps during its 22–23 March meeting. While the Federal Reserve noted that inflation remains high,

---

2 Schneider, Howard. 2023. Fed's Waller Sees No Signs of 'Quick' Decline in Inflation. *Reuters*. 9 February.

it softened its hawkish language. The Federal Reserve said that it had considered keeping rates steady in light of the recent banking turmoil and removed the phrase "ongoing rate increases" from its policy statement. In addition, the Federal Reserve updated forecasts in March from those made in December with a slight downgrade to GDP forecasts for 2023 (to 0.4% from 0.5%) and 2024 (to 1.2% from 1.6%). The PCE inflation projection for 2023 was slightly increased (to 3.3% from 3.1%). The expected terminal federal funds rate was unchanged for 2023 and 2025, but increased for 2024 (to 4.3% from 4.1%). Based on the Federal Reserve's forecasts, one more interest rate hike of 25 bps is expected in 2023 before a pause.

Meanwhile, the US economic outlook remained dim. Annualized gross domestic product (GDP) growth weakened to 2.7% in the fourth quarter (Q4) of 2022 from 3.2% in the third quarter (Q3). While unemployment remained low in Q4 2022, nonfarm payroll additions posted continuous declines from 350,000 in September to 324,000 in October, 290,000 in November, and 260,000 in December. The risk of recession abated somewhat following the strong nonfarm payroll report of 504,000 new additions in January 2023 and a higher-than-expected 311,000 additions in February 2023.

Similarly, the European Central Bank (ECB) continued to tighten its monetary stance to ease inflation, albeit at a moderated pace. Inflation in the euro area has trended downward yet remains elevated. Inflation peaked in October at 10.6% y-o-y, then gradually eased to 10.1% y-o-y, 9.2% y-o-y, 8.6% y-o-y, and 8.5% y-o-y in November, December, January, and February, respectively. GDP growth also softened to 1.9% y-o-y in Q4 2022 from 2.5% y-o-y in Q3 2022. On 15 December, the ECB raised its key policy rates by 50 bps, which was less than the 75 bps rate hike announced on 27 October. Meanwhile, the ECB announced a reduction in its Asset Purchase Programme holdings by EUR15 billion each month from March 2023 to June 2023, before it plans to reassess its balance sheet reduction program. On 2 February and 16 March, the ECB raised policy rates by 50 bps each, as expected. The ECB also released updated economic forecasts in March. However, the ECB noted that these were made prior to the recent banking sector turmoil, adding uncertainty to these forecasts.

The ECB raised its forecast for 2023 GDP growth in the euro area to 1.0% in March from 0.5% in December,

but lowered its growth forecasts for 2024 to 1.6% from 1.9%, and for 2025 to 1.6% from 1.8%. It also reduced its inflation projections in March for 2023, 2024, and 2025 to 5.3%, 2.9%, and 2.1%, respectively, from 6.3%, 3.4%, and 2.3%.

In Japan, inflation has been steadily increasing and the BOJ has largely maintained the monetary stance. Japan's consumer price inflation rose from 3.0% y-o-y in September to 3.7% y-o-y in October, 3.8% y-o-y in November, 4.0% y-o-y in December, and 4.3% y-o-y in January. GDP growth accelerated to an annualized 0.1% in Q4 2022, reversing Q3 2022's 1.1% decline. During its 20 December meeting, the BOJ kept its key policy rates unchanged but widened the trading band of Japanese Government Bonds from ±0.25% to ±0.50%. Although the BOJ indicated this does not suggest monetary tightening, the market largely interpreted it as a pivot in the BOJ's monetary policy. This decision raised expectations that the BOJ would eventually shift its accommodative monetary stance. On 18 January, the BOJ left its monetary policy unchanged and revised downward its GDP growth forecasts to 1.9%, 1.7%, and 1.1% for fiscal years 2022, 2023, and 2024, respectively, from October forecasts of 2.0%, 1.9%, and 1.5%. The BOJ also revised its inflation forecasts for fiscal years 2022, 2023, and 2024 to 3.0%, 1.6%, and 1.8%, respectively, from corresponding October projections of 2.9%, 1.6%, and 1.6%. The BOJ noted that short-term inflation is being driven by the pass-through effect of high commodity prices, which is expected to wane. During its 9–10 March monetary policy meeting, the BOJ maintained its existing monetary policy, keeping policy rates unchanged and the trading band of Japanese Government Bonds at ±0.5%. The move reduced market expectations that the BOJ would be pivoting to a tighter monetary policy.

In a majority of emerging East Asia markets, 10-year government bond yields fell during the review period. This trend was largely supported by moderating monetary tightening in major advanced economies, as well as declining inflation in many regional economies (**Figure A**). The 10-year bond yield in the Philippines witnessed the largest decline of 86 bps, with a 109 bps decline recorded in December–January on expectations that the central bank would ease its monetary tightening in 2023 through moderating rate hikes and a reduction in reserve requirement ratios.[3] The decline was partly reversed by increases in bond yields from 1 February

---

[3] Morales, Neil Jerome. 2023. Philippines C.bank Flags 25 or 50 bps Rate Hike Next Month. *Reuters*. 10 January.

Figure A: Inflation in Select Emerging East Asian Markets

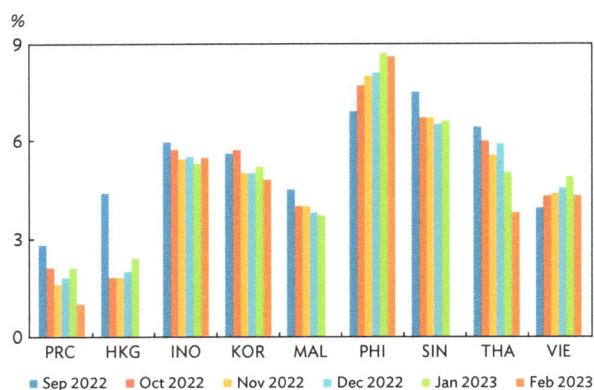

HKG = Hong Kong, China; INO = Indonesia; KOR = Korea, Rep. of; MAL = Malaysia; PHI = Philippines; PRC = China, People's Rep. of; SIN = Singapore; THA = Thailand; VIE = Viet Nam.
Note: Data coverage is from September 2022 to February 2023 except for Hong Kong, China; Malaysia; and Singapore (January 2023).
Sources: Various local sources.

through 10 March, as inflation continued to rise and the Bangko Sentral ng Pilipinas surprised markets with a 50 bps rate hike on 16 February. It followed this up with a smaller 25 bps rate hike on 23 March as inflation remained high with slight decline in February. Viet Nam witnessed the second-largest decline in its 10-year bond yield during the review period, which was partly driven by risk aversion in corporate bond markets. Investors flocked to government bonds for safety amid stress in the corporate bond market, where many real estate companies face liquidity constraints in meeting debt obligations. On 14 March, the State Bank of Vietnam left unchanged its refinancing rate but reduced its discount rate and overnight rate by 100 bps each to support economic growth and ease liquidity stress in financial markets.

Regional financial conditions generally improved during the review period. Most improvements happened in December 2022 and January 2023 on moderating monetary tightening in advanced economies, easing inflationary pressures in the region, and boosted investor sentiment over the economic benefits of the reopening of the People's Republic of China (PRC) economy. **Box 1** suggests a sound economic outlook for emerging East Asia in 2023.

During the review period, a majority of emerging East Asian currencies strengthened against the US dollar.

Regional currencies appreciated by an average of 1.3% (simple) and 2.1% (GDP-weighted). The strengthening largely happened in December and January, when average appreciations of 3.9% (simple) and 5.0% (GDP-weighted) were posted. From 1 February to 10 March, most regional currencies weakened against the US dollar, with an average depreciation of 2.5% (simple) and 2.7% (GDP-weighted) (**Figure B**). Risk premiums, gauged by credit default swap spreads, also trended downward during the review period, posting a GDP-weighted average narrowing of 3 bps (**Figure C**). The reduction of risk premiums was more pronounced in December–January, followed by widening risk premiums from 1 February to 10 March in several economies.

The souring of investment sentiment in February and early March was more pronounced in equity markets. During the review period, regional equity markets posted a market-weighted average return of 1.6%, driven by strong gains in the PRC and Hong Kong, China. Excluding the PRC and Hong Kong, China, regional equity markets posted a market-weighted loss of 3.1% (**Figure D**). Regional equity markets rallied 5.7% (market-weighted) in December–January, but retreated 3.6% from 1 February to 10 March over uncertainties in the direction of the Federal Reserve's monetary stance (**Figure E**). The biggest gain was seen in the Lao People's Democratic Republic (Lao PDR), which rose 31.9% during the review period as the reopening of the PRC is expected to boost economic activities through the Lao PDR–PRC railway. The equity markets of both Hong Kong, China and the PRC posted gains during the review period, rising 2.5% and 3.9%, respectively, following the reopening of the PRC's economy.

The region's equity markets experienced strong net portfolio inflows of USD31.9 billion from 30 November 2022 to 10 March 2023 (**Figure F**). Of this total, USD27.9 billion went to the PRC following the economy's reopening. The Republic of Korea received USD5.3 billion of inflows on expectations of possible inclusion in Morgan Stanley Capital International's developed market index this year. In addition, financial regulators in the Republic of Korea are planning to relax regulations to make investing in the stock market easier for offshore investors. In contrast, ASEAN economies posted aggregate net foreign equity outflows of USD1.2 billion during the review period. This was largely driven by Indonesia's net outflows of USD1.1 billion following the decision of the government to curb palm oil exports to

Box 1: Economic Outlook in Developing Asia

Growth in developing Asia remained strong in 2022.[a] Robust domestic activity underpinned by reopening offset the negative impact from a worsening global economy; the slowdown in the People's Republic of China (PRC); and policy rate hikes across the region, triggered by rising inflation and aggressive monetary tightening in the United States (US).

External headwinds will continue to be significant this year. Oil prices are forecast to remain elevated. Growth in advanced economies will slow, as above-target inflation leads to tighter financial conditions. Recent indicators, however, suggest that economic activity in the PRC is picking up and may prove more resilient than expected in the US and euro area. In addition, the global economy is set to receive a boost from a growth rebound in the PRC once the current coronavirus disease (COVID-19) wave is over.

Against this backdrop, recovery in developing Asia is projected to lose some steam as the effects of reopening wane—but it will remain solid. In December, the Asian Development Bank trimmed the region's growth forecast for 2023 by 0.3 percentage points to 4.6% (**Table B1**). A challenging global outlook is expected to slow expansion in every subregion but the Caucasus and Central Asia, which has fared better than

expected on positive spillovers from the Russian invasion of Ukraine. The forecast for regional inflation this year is 4.2%, with higher inflation expected for South Asia, Southeast Asia, and the Pacific. Despite the downgraded growth forecast, developing Asia is still projected to grow more than most other regions—and suffer lower inflation.

Developing Asia faces several risks but also opportunities. In the short term, an escalation of the Russian invasion of Ukraine could renew surges in commodity prices, stoking global inflation and inducing further monetary tightening. Inflationary pressures in the US and other advanced economies could prove more persistent than expected, prolonging the current monetary tightening cycle. On the other hand, more rapid disinflation could lead to a quicker pivot toward policy rate cuts, supporting a rebound in economic activity and financial markets.

The main upside risks and opportunities, however, are associated with reopening in the PRC, which may be a turning point for developing Asia. A smooth exit from pandemic-related policies and resolution of property market issues in the PRC could brighten regional economic prospects—boosting exports, consumption, and investment.

Table B1: Gross Domestic Product Growth and Inflation Forecasts (% per year)

| | | GDP Growth | | | | | Inflation | | | |
| | | 2022 | | 2023 | | | 2022 | | 2023 | |
	2021	September Update	December ADOS	September Update	December ADOS	2021	September Update	December ADOS	September Update	December ADOS
Developing Asia	7.0	4.3	4.2	4.9	4.6	2.5	4.5	4.4	4.0	4.2
Caucasus and Central Asia	5.7	3.9	4.8	4.2	4.2	8.9	11.5	12.5	8.5	8.5
East Asia	7.7	3.2	2.9	4.2	4.0	1.1	2.5	2.4	2.5	2.4
South Asia	8.1	6.5	6.5	6.5	6.3	5.8	8.1	8.2	7.4	7.9
Southeast Asia	3.3	5.1	5.5	5.0	4.7	2.0	5.2	5.1	4.1	4.5
The Pacific	(1.7)	4.7	5.3	5.5	4.8	3.1	6.2	5.8	4.8	5.0

( ) = negative, ADOS = *Asian Development Outlook Supplement*, GDP = gross domestic product.
Source: *Asian Development Outlook* database (accessed 7 March 2023).

---

[a] This box was written by Irfan Qureshi (economist) and David de Padua (economics officer) in the Economic Research and Regional Cooperation Department of the Asian Development Bank.

focus on domestic supply, which may impact Indonesia's trade surplus.[4]

The region's bond markets recorded aggregate net foreign portfolio inflows of USD1.7 billion in December

2022 and January 2023 (**Figure G**). Most regional bond markets posted inflows, with the exceptions being the Republic of Korea and Malaysia. The Republic of Korea posted net outflows of USD8.6 billion from its bond market as a sizable volume of bonds matured and

---

[4] Thukral, Naveen, and Bernadette Christina. 2023. Indonesia Palm Oil Export Curbs, Biodiesel Plans to Hit World Vegoil Supplies. *Reuters*. 16 January.

Figure B: Changes in Select Emerging East Asian Currencies

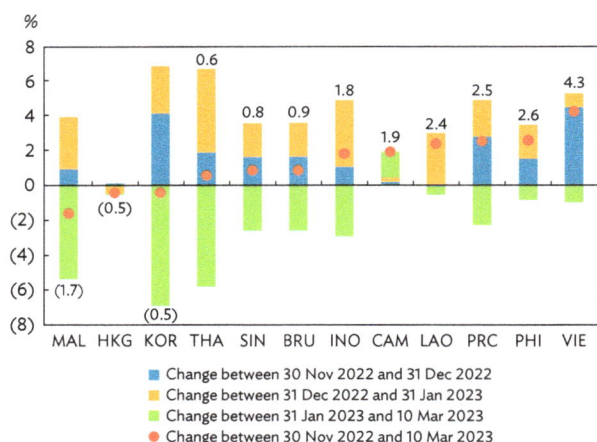

( ) = negative; BRU = Brunei Darussalam; CAM = Cambodia; HKG = Hong Kong, China; INO = Indonesia; KOR = Korea, Rep. of; LAO = Lao People's Democratic Republic; MAL = Malaysia; PHI = Philippines; PRC = China, People's Rep. of; SIN = Singapore; THA = Thailand; VIE = Viet Nam.

Notes:
1. A positive (negative) value for the foreign exchange rate indicates the appreciation (depreciation) of the local currency against the United States dollar.
2. Figures refer to change between 30 November 2022 and 10 March 2023.

Source: *AsianBondsOnline* computations based on Bloomberg LP data.

Figure D: Changes in Select Emerging East Asian Equity Indices

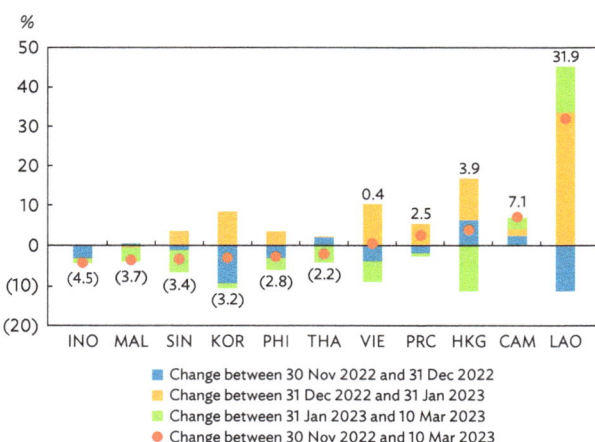

( ) = negative; CAM = Cambodia; PRC = China, People's Rep. of; HKG = Hong Kong, China; INO = Indonesia; KOR = Korea, Rep. of; LAO = Lao People's Democratic Republic; MAL = Malaysia; PHI = Philippines; SIN = Singapore; THA = Thailand; VIE = Viet Nam.

Note: Figures refer to change between 30 November 2022 and 10 March 2023.

Source: *AsianBondsOnline* computations based on Bloomberg LP data.

Figure C: Changes in Credit Default Swap Spreads in Select Emerging East Asian Markets (senior 5-year)

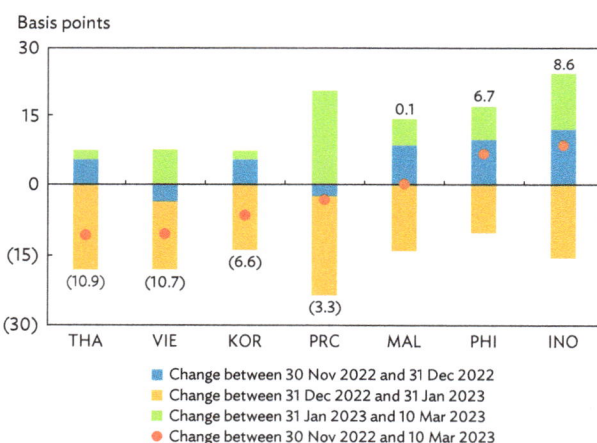

( ) = negative; INO = Indonesia; KOR = Korea, Rep. of; MAL = Malaysia; PHI = Philippines; PRC = China, People's Rep. of; THA = Thailand; VIE = Viet Nam.

Note: Figures refer to change between 30 November 2022 and 10 March 2023.

Source: *AsianBondsOnline* computations based on Bloomberg LP data.

investors anticipated that the Bank of Korea was nearing the end of its tightening cycle. In Malaysia, there were small net capital outflows of USD0.1 billion during the 2-month review period. Among the remaining regional bond markets, Indonesia recorded the largest net inflows at USD5.0 billion due to its attractive yields. The PRC recorded the region's second-largest net foreign capital inflows of USD2.6 billion. Meanwhile, the Thai bond market received USD2.5 billion of foreign capital inflows over optimism that the PRC's reopening would boost tourism receipts. **Box 2** discusses investment opportunities in ASEAN bond markets.

Overall, the outlook for emerging East Asia's financial conditions remains benign as recession fears and inflation have eased and some regional central banks are expected to end their tightening cycles. Investors see many opportunities in global bond markets in 2023. **Box 3** discusses the return of investor demand for bonds. However, the outlook is far from certain and remains largely driven by a few key risk factors.

Figure E: Movements in Equity Indexes in Select Emerging East Asian Markets

1 January 2022 = 100

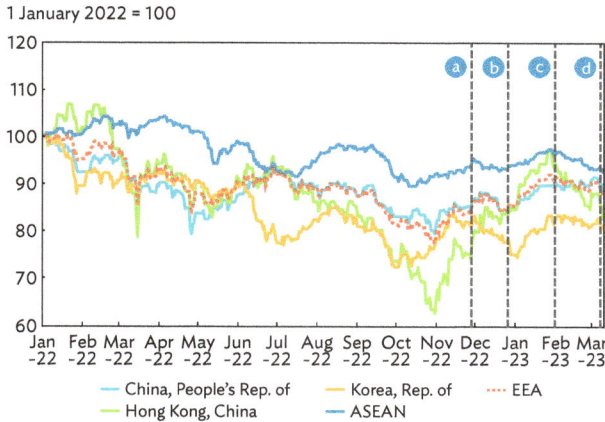

ASEAN = Association of Southeast Asian Nations, EEA = emerging East Asia, FOMC = Federal Open Market Committee, PRC = People's Republic of China, US = United States.

a Market expectations of slowing Federal Reserve rate hikes in antipation of Chairman Powell's speech at Brookings Institution
b The PRC announced the lifting of quarantine requirements for international arrivals
c January FOMC meeting
d Chairman Powell's semi-annual report to Congress noted that interest rates will likely rise more than expected

Notes:
1. Equity market indexes included in ASEAN are the Jakarta Stock Exchange Composite Index, Kuala Lumpur Composite Index, Philippine Stock Exchange Index, Straits Times Index, Stock Exchange of Thailand Index, and Vietnam Ho Chi Minh Stock Index.
2. Data as of 10 March 2023.
3. Emerging East Asia is defined to include member states of the Association of Southeast Asian Nations (ASEAN) plus the People's Republic of China; Hong Kong, China; and the Republic of Korea.

Sources: *AsianBondsOnline* computations based on Bloomberg LP data; Marte, Jonnelle. 2022. Powell to Set Stage for Slowing Fed Rate Hikes Amid Hawkish Tone. *Bloomberg.* 28 November; and Schneider, Howard, and Ann Saphir. 2022. Fed's Powell: Rate Hikes to Slow, but Adjustment Just Beginning. *Reuters.* 1 December.

Figure F: Foreign Capital Flows in Equity Markets in Select Emerging East Asian Markets

USD billion

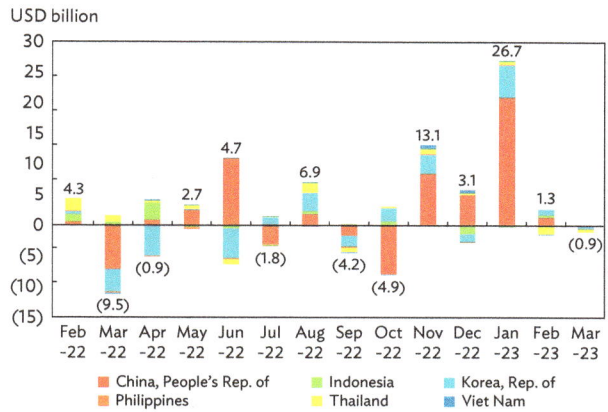

( ) = outflows, USD = United States dollar.

Notes:
1. Data coverage is from 1 February 2022 to 10 March 2023.
2. Figures refer to net inflows (net outflows) for each month.
3. Emerging East Asia is defined to include member states of the Association of Southeast Asian Nations (ASEAN) plus the People's Republic of China; Hong Kong, China; and the Republic of Korea.

Source: Institute of International Finance.

Figure G: Foreign Capital Flows in Local Currency Bond Markets in Select Emerging East Asian Markets

USD billion

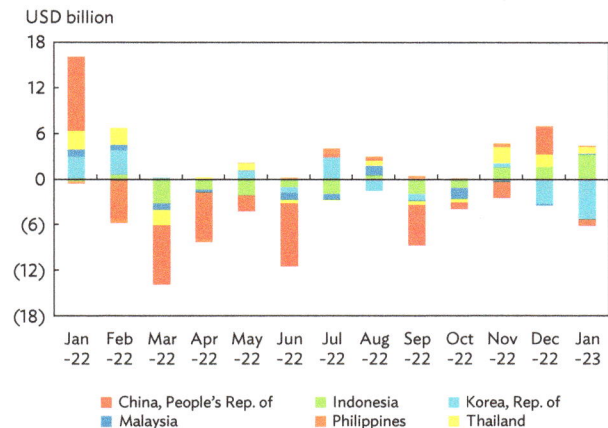

( ) = negative, USD = United States dollar.

Notes:
1. The Republic of Korea and Thailand provided data on bond flows. For the People's Republic of China, Indonesia, Malaysia, and the Philippines, month-on-month changes in foreign holdings of local currency government bonds were used as a proxy for bond flows.
2. Data are as of 31 January 2023.
3. Figures were computed based on 31 January 2023 exchange rates and do not include currency effects.
4. Emerging East Asia is defined to include member states of the Association of Southeast Asian Nations (ASEAN) plus the People's Republic of China; Hong Kong, China; and the Republic of Korea.

Sources: People's Republic of China (Bloomberg LP); Indonesia (Directorate General of Budget Financing and Risk Management, Ministry of Finance); Republic of Korea (Financial Supervisory Service); Malaysia (Bank Negara Malaysia); Philippines (Bureau of the Treasury); and Thailand (Thai Bond Market Association).

First is the uncertain pace of monetary tightening in advanced economies. The Federal Reserve in its March projections indicated that it will take a pause after one more rate hike in 2023.[5] However, uncertainty in inflation and development of current banking sector turmoil would affect the path of monetary policy, casting uncertainty over financial conditions in the region.

Second, a US dollar strengthened by the Federal Reserve's monetary tightening can challenge financial stability and debt sustainability in emerging markets economies. **Box 4** discusses these debt sustainability risks in emerging markets amid dollar fluctuations.

---

[5] Federal Reserve. 2023. Summary of Economic Projections. *FOMC Projection Materials.* 21–22 March.

Box 2: Investors' View—Opportunities and Risks for Private Investors in ASEAN Local Currency Bond Markets

Central banks overseeing the 10 most heavily traded currencies delivered a combined 2,700 basis points of tightening through 54 rate hikes in 2022.[a] While the World Bank and International Monetary Fund predicted that we saw the peak of inflation in 2022 in their January 2023 *Global Economic Prospects* and *World Economic Outlook* reports, respectively, the future path of major benchmark interest rates is far from certain.

Against this global backdrop, this box discusses what global investors should keep in mind when investing in emerging East Asian local currency (LCY) government bond markets in 2023. The Indonesian market offers relative stability and decent returns. Investments in Thailand have the highest exposure to currency fluctuations and policy rate adjustments. Investors' confidence in Malaysia depends on political actions to rein in rising national debt.

Globally, emerging economies with higher exposure to foreign currency financing are the most impacted by higher interest rates in the United States (US) and a stronger US dollar, as they need to pay more just to service their debt.

Neither of the two Association of Southeast Asian Nations (ASEAN) economies in the frontier market category, Cambodia and the Lao People's Democratic Republic (Lao PDR), have a properly functioning LCY bond market. Further, most of their debts are held by external lenders such as multilateral development banks and the People's Republic of China. The big difference from international investors' point of view between the two economies is that, while Cambodia has experienced relatively low single-digit inflation and a stable exchange rate over the last 2 years, the Lao PDR's inflation started rising significantly in the middle of 2022 and hit 39.3% in December, with the Lao kip losing over 50% in value against the US dollar last year. A recently released case study from the Asian Development Bank highlights how the development of the LCY government bond market in the Lao PDR could help facilitate economic recovery and build resilience against future shocks.[b]

All five emerging markets in ASEAN have seen relative stability in their respective LCY government bond markets

over the last 2 years, with the 10-year benchmark yield's volatility in each economy comfortably below the market turmoil levels experienced during the second quarter of 2020 (**Figure B2.1**). Souring sentiment in global emerging markets in the third quarter of 2022 had bigger impacts on credit default swaps spreads, currency exchange rates, and equity markets than on LCY government bonds.

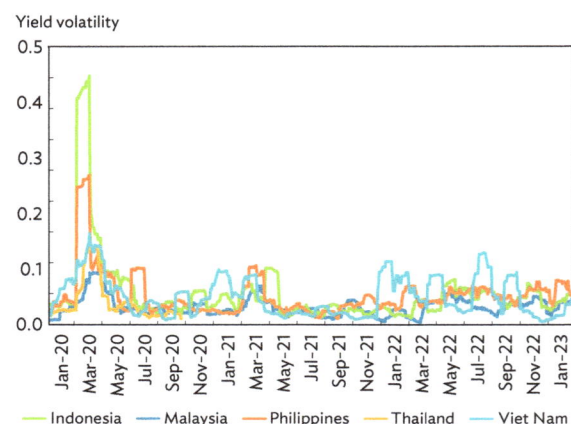

Figure B2.1: Local Currency Bond Yield Volatility in Emerging ASEAN Economies

ASEAN = Association of Southeast Asian Nations.
Source: AsianBondsOnline calculations based on Bloomberg LP data (accessed 16 February 2023).

Indonesia continued its efforts to promote domestic investment and stabilize capital flows in 2022, which resulted in the most significant reduction of the foreign holdings share in the LCY government bond market among the five economies included in **Figure B2.2**. In the last 3 years, Indonesia has managed to increase the overall size of its LCY government bond market—now the biggest among emerging markets in ASEAN by a wide margin—while keeping the 10-year benchmark yield in an attractive and stable range of 6%–8%. Increased participation from domestic financial institutions provides a cushion against capital outflows in times of heightened financial tensions, as examined in Box 1: Foreign Participation in Asian Local Currency Bond Markets and Financial Stability Risks in the March 2022 edition of the *Asia Bond Monitor*.[c]

---

[a] This box was written by Krzysztof Rojek (senior director) of Global Solutions Consulting, Finastra. The views expressed in this box are those of the author and do not necessarily reflect the views of Finastra. Data have been sourced from the *AsianBondsOnline* Data Portal.

[b] Yamadera, Satoru, and Kengo Mizuno. 2022. *Developing a Local Currency Government Bond Market in an Emerging Economy after COVID-19: Case for the Lao People's Democratic Republic.* https://www.adb.org/sites/default/files/publication/845376/local-currency-government-bond-market-lao-pdr.pdf.

[c] Beirne, John, and Ulrich Volz. 2022. Box 1: Foreign Participation in Asian Local Currency Bond Markets and Financial Stability Risks. *Asia Bond Monitor* March 2022. pp. 16–18. https://asianbondsonline.adb.org/documents/abm/abm_mar_2022_global_regional_market_developments.pdf.

continued on next page

Box 2 *continued*

Figure B2.2: Foreign Holdings in Local Currency Government Bond Markets in Emerging ASEAN Economies

% of total

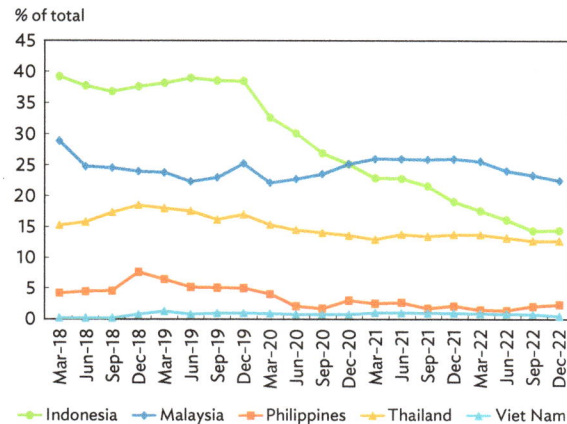

ASEAN = Association of Southeast Asian Nations.

Source: *AsianBondsOnline* calculations based on various local sources (accessed 16 February 2023).

Thailand has the lowest policy rate and bond yields among the five ASEAN economies included in Figure B2.2. As the economy with the highest level of dependency on tourism, Thailand looks forward to increased tourist arrivals in 2023, partly driven by the reopening of the People's Republic of China. Thailand has increased its 2023 growth forecast from 2.8% to 3.6%. The risk–return profile is not ideal for the Thai LCY bond market though, with low returns to begin with and two major risks to the downside: (i) the volatility of the Thai baht due to rate differentials, and (ii) another potential spike in energy prices that could upset the policy rate and impact domestic bond yields.

Malaysia faces rapidly rising national debt that needs to be addressed. Newly elected Prime Minister Anwar Ibrahim has promised to take action that will restore investors' confidence in Malaysia. The new budget, which had yet to be proposed at the time of writing, and how new policies are implemented are the most important factors for global investors to watch.

The Philippines and Viet Nam have the region's two smallest LCY government bond markets along with negligible foreign holding shares of 2.3% and 0.5%, respectively. The Philippines has a significant foreign currency government bond market, while Viet Nam's LCY bonds outstanding are owned primarily by domestic banks and insurance and pension funds. Viet Nam's corporate bond market is exhibiting signs of stress, and there are concerns that professional investors are unlikely to return to the market this year due to Decree 65's restrictions and high new issuance costs.[d]

In conclusion, ASEAN bond markets have fared the recent global market turmoil better than either foreign exchange or equity markets. ASEAN LCY government bonds offer relatively more stability than those in other emerging economies in Asia and the world. There are good investment opportunities in the region, both for those who are conservative (Indonesia) and brave (Thailand, if currency exposure is unhedged). Last, but not least, it is very important to closely follow political and regulatory changes, especially in Malaysia and Viet Nam, as new opportunities may emerge very quickly and those who capture them first will benefit the most.

[d] Decree 65 stipulates that issuers may no longer use bonds to increase capital or restructure capital sources except for the restructuring of their own debt. Issuers may only issue bonds for the implementation of investment plans and investment projects, or for restructuring their own debt.

Box 3: 2023—A Tale of Two Halves for Credit Markets

Sharp repricing and extreme volatility shook bond markets in 2022 after central banks' abrupt monetary policy tightening.[a] Today, markets are navigating a high degree of uncertainty, and bonds are back in focus. More attractive yields and less rate volatility restored demand for the asset class at the turn of the year (**Figure B3.1**). Amundi expects this trend to continue throughout 2023, which we see as a two-speed year for credit markets.

Figure B3.1: Appealing Yields in Credit Markets

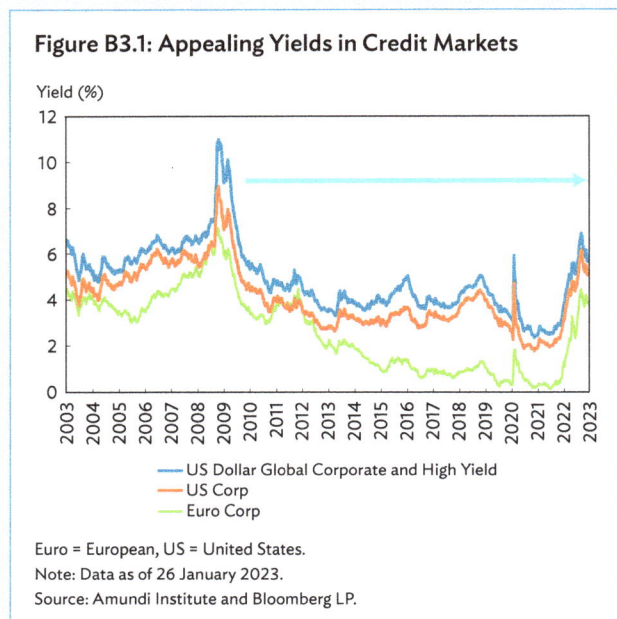

Yield (%)

Euro = European, US = United States.
Note: Data as of 26 January 2023.
Source: Amundi Institute and Bloomberg LP.

Global Backdrop

Our baseline scenario for 2023 is one of sluggish global economic growth (2.4%) and protracted high inflation (5.8%). Despite recent signs of moderation in headline inflation, the United States (US) Federal Reserve and the European Central Bank (ECB) are keen to fight inflation and avoid excessive easing of financing conditions. In the US, we think the Federal Reserve would tolerate a recession in order to bring down inflation. In the euro area, we will carefully monitor how the ECB will balance inflation expectations and financial stability risk should energy prices remain persistently high. We forecast the Federal Reserve's terminal rate at 5.25% and the ECB's at 3.50%.

Investor concerns will gradually shift from inflation and rates to the economic slowdown. Volatility in equity markets should therefore become the main driver of credit markets, with increasing focus on differentiating across sectors and individual companies to capture the rebound that will follow.

Credit Quality has Probably Peaked, Despite Healthier Corporate Balance Sheets

Corporate balance sheet positions have generally improved since 2020. Low refinancing needs and high use of cash holdings limited the negative impact of monetary tightening on corporate balance sheets in both the US and Europe. Issuers also took advantage of exceptional financing conditions, with primary market activity hitting record levels. Today, despite falling cash levels, net leverage is overall below pre-coronavirus disease (COVID-19) levels, and corporates have also improved their debt duration and credit metrics.

However, the peak in credit quality is probably behind us. Corporates are now facing a more challenging environment. In 2023, sluggish growth, rising energy prices, and higher funding and business costs should result in increased high-yield (HY) default rates. A benign redemption schedule will mitigate these factors, in particular during the first half of the year when relatively few issues are due.

We do not expect higher debt costs to overwhelm investment grade (IG) issuers, but refinancing concerns may pressure financially weaker issuers in the second half of the year. HY default rates may rise close to their historic average by the end of 2023, nearing 5% in the US and 4% in the euro area (**Figure B3.2**).

Attractive Investment-Grade Valuations and High-Yield Opportunities in 2023

Despite the recent rally in corporate bonds markets, the general backdrop still provides opportunities for global credit investors actively monitoring specific bottom-up risks.

Overall, we favor IG over HY, as we believe the HY–IG spread will widen in 2023. In our view, the HY spread compression in 2022 was technically driven since the segment experienced one of its lowest cumulated issuance in several years (**Figure B3.3**).

---

[a] This box was written by Monica Defend (head) of Amundi Institute. The write up is based on Defend, Monica, and Amaury D'Orsay. 2023. "Bonds are Back: Credit Markets in Focus During 2023." *Amundi Institute*. 26 January.

continued on next page

Box 3 *continued*

Figure B3.2: Default Outlook, United States and European High-Yield

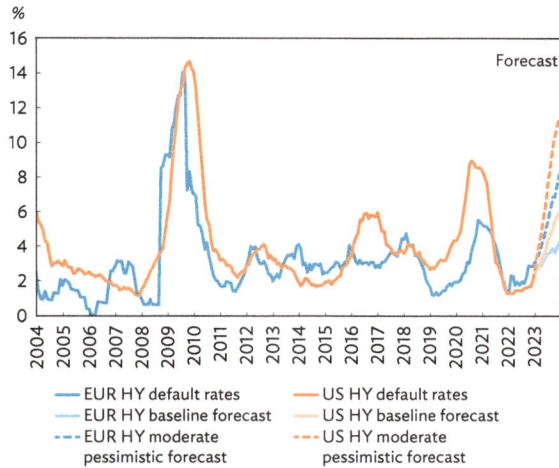

EUR = euro, HY = high-yield, US = United States.
Note: Data as of 25 January 2023. Forecasts start from January 2023.
Source: Amundi Institute and Moody's.

Figure B3.3: European–United States High-Yield Spread Differential

euro = European, US = United States.
Note: Data as of 20 January 2023.
Source: Amundi Institute and BofA Indices.

In the IG segment, our preference goes to EUR- and GBP-denominated debt over US credit. The former are very cheap by historical standards and current spread levels reflect a far bleaker backdrop than what we expect. We also see value in EUR-subordinated debt, where absolute yields currently compensate for potential volatility and should create opportunities.

On a sectoral basis, we favor financials, especially banks, over nonfinancials. For nonfinancials, we hold positive views on the auto, technology, media, and telecom sectors, but we are cautious on consumer goods, capital goods, and transportation.

The HY segment is attractive on a mid-term investment horizon as spreads should be volatile throughout the year. We currently maintain a cautious stance but believe opportunities will materialize in the second half of 2023 when uncertainty over monetary policy fades.

Mixed Picture for Technicals

To conclude, more attractive yields and lower risks have improved the technical backdrop for credit markets. Fresh inflows materialized after many months of outflows, with less defensive investors across the board seeing fixed income, including IG credit, as a diversifier.

On the supply side, we expect net supply to increase in 2023, with higher issuance than in 2022 when the HY primary market was almost closed. However, 2023 net supply should remain modest by historical standards.

In the euro area, we expect the ECB to start its quantitative tightening in March. We also expect this to have a limited impact on markets. Corporate debt volumes are on the rise, but the volumes announced for the ECB's Asset Purchase Programme and Corporate Sector Purchase Programme redemptions are overall modest.

Finally, investors should look at opportunities in green bonds and other sustainable debt instruments. The market for labeled bonds has continuously grown, reaching EUR700 billion in 2022. It is expected to rise further and offer attractive opportunities as central banks take actions to decarbonize their balance sheets. Green bonds also tend to exhibit lower volatility than conventional bonds, while sustainability-linked bonds are typically forward-looking, performance-based instruments that can bring diversification to the issuer base without compromising yield.

Box 4: United States Dollar Fluctuations and Debt Sustainability Risks in Emerging Market Economies

A tightening United States (US) monetary policy cycle in 2022 in the face of severe inflationary pressures led to a broad-based appreciation of the US dollar for most of the year.[a] This raised concerns about debt sustainability in emerging market economies (EMEs) as borrowing costs rose and external debt servicing obligations amplified. Sharp fluctuations in US dollar exchange rates also have well-documented negative implications for the EME growth outlook (e.g., Hofmann and Park 2020). While the US dollar depreciated somewhat at the end of 2022 and the start of 2023, it remained at a relatively high level over the 12-month period from January 2022 to January 2023.

From January through October 2022, EME currencies depreciated relative to the US dollar by around 10% on average, including in Association of Southeast Asian Nations economies. As global commodity prices rose during the year, net commodity exporters largely experienced less severe depreciations, benefiting from dollar-invoiced export revenue, while the currencies of some commodity-exporting Latin American countries actually strengthened. Advanced economies were also affected, including depreciations for the euro and the Japanese yen, among others. Toward the end of 2022, market expectations of less aggressive US monetary policy tightening due to easing domestic inflation, as well as smaller US Federal Reserve rate hikes, led to a depreciation of the US dollar, particularly from November 2022 to January 2023 (**Figure B4.1**).

To set some context for recent developments, in the latter part of 2022 the US dollar reached its highest level since the aftermath of the 9/11 terrorist attacks in 2001 (**Figure B4.2**). The appreciation of the dollar since the Russian invasion of Ukraine in February 2022 reflected higher yields in the US as it combatted inflation, which was in part driven by rising food and energy commodity prices as well as the post-pandemic US recovery in demand. In November 2022, dollar depreciation took hold as US inflation eased, and the currency fell 5% month-on-month relative to a global basket of currencies. While downward pressure on the dollar continued through January 2023, the dollar overall remained strong relative to its level in January 2022. Therefore, while there is some respite for EME debt exposures given recent downward shifts in the dollar, debt sustainability risks remain elevated.

Figure B4.1: Global Exchange Rate Changes Relative to the United States Dollar

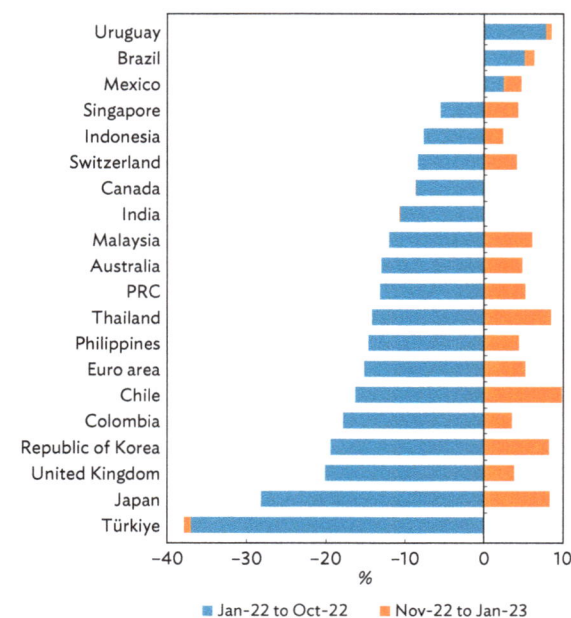

PRC = People's Republic of China.
Note: Reported are the nominal bilateral United States (US) dollar exchange rate changes (monthly averages). Negative values imply a depreciation relative to the US dollar.
Source: Bank for International Settlements database (accessed 7 February 2023).

Macroeconomic Challenges and Debt Sustainability Risks

Higher yields in the US during 2022, in conjunction with amplified global risk aversion and uncertainty, led to a flow of capital into US dollar-denominated assets (International Monetary Fund 2022). While many EMEs, particularly in Asia, are more resilient to external shocks than in the past given stronger macroeconomic fundamentals and more favorable current account positions, recent developments pose challenges in managing capital flows, with record levels of emerging market bond fund outflows taking place during 2022.

Rising commodity prices during 2022 weighed further on the currencies of net commodity importers given that commodities are priced in US dollars, thereby negatively

---

[a] This box was written by John Beirne (vice-chair of research and senior research fellow) and Pradeep Panthi (research associate) of the Asian Development Bank Institute.

continued on next page

Box 4   *continued*

Figure B4.2: United States Dollar Fluctuations, 1985–2023

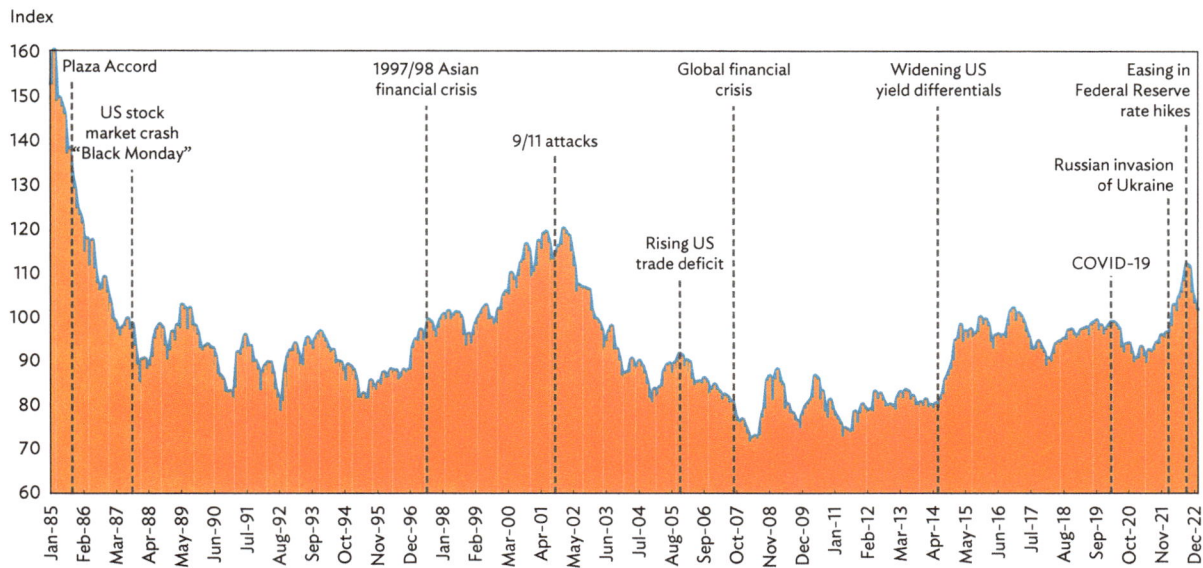

COVID-19 = coronavirus disease, US = United States.
Note: Reported is the United States (US) Dollar Index Chart from January 1985 to January 2023 (monthly), which measures the value of the US dollar relative to a basket of other currencies.
Source: Bloomberg LP data.

affecting trade balances. Economies that have high levels of external debt denominated in US dollars were particularly exposed, with debt sustainability threatened by surges in the local currency value of the debt and rising debt servicing costs. For EMEs globally, with the exception of emerging European economies, over 80% of external debt is denominated in US dollars. In this context, compared to other regions, emerging and developing Asia has a lower share of external debt to gross domestic product (**Figure B4.3**). Therefore, while emerging and developing Asia remains exposed to US dollar appreciation in terms of external debt risks, it is less exposed than other regions.

Policy Options for Emerging Market Economies

While EMEs face inflationary pressures related to supply chain disruptions resulting from the Russian invasion of Ukraine that have amplified energy and food commodity prices, tightening domestic monetary policies in EMEs during 2022 prevented higher imported inflation via currency depreciation relative to the US dollar and also mitigated against sharp net capital outflows. This came at the risk of weakening the growth outlook, however, especially through rising costs of

Figure B4.3: Total External Debt as a Share of Gross Domestic Product, 2022

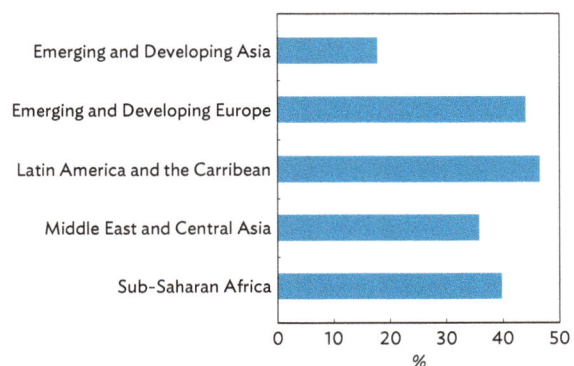

Note: The economies included in each region are per the International Monetary Fund's regional classification system.
Source: International Monetary Fund. 2022. *World Economic Outlook*. October. Washington, DC.

continued on next page

Box 4   *continued*

borrowing and threats to debt sustainability, which could also hamper investment. While Asian EMEs overall have a more robust growth outlook for 2023 than other EME regions, there remains significant intra-regional heterogeneity.

To defend their currencies against excessive depreciation, as well as raising rates, many EMEs intervened in foreign exchange markets during 2022, selling US dollars from foreign reserves and buying domestic currency. Asian EMEs—including India, Indonesia, the Phillipines, and Thailand—reinforced the impact of raising interest rates in their economies with such interventions, also helping to stem capital outflows. While an important tool for addressing financial market functioning and inflation expectations risks, the adequacy of reserve holdings needs to be considered in the context of ensuring that external debt servicing obligations are not compromised. Further, an abrupt and substantial depletion of foreign exchange reserves, while supporting the domestic currency, could have negative implications for sovereign credit rating assessments (e.g., Mohanty and Berger 2013, Disyatat and Galati 2007).

In the short term, EMEs should continue to manage inflationary pressures through well-coordinated domestic monetary and fiscal policies, in particular by ensuring that fiscal policies aimed at mitigating the effects of cost-push inflation do not aggravate inflation expectations. Further easing of inflation in the US during 2023 would also trigger less aggressive US monetary policy tightening and dollar weakening, implying less amplified risks to debt sustainability in EMEs. Over the longer term, while borrowing in US dollar-denominated debt will continue to be necessary for many EMEs, policies should aim to reduce exposure to abrupt US dollar fluctuations. This can include debt restructuring and debt servicing schemes that feature currency hedging

components, as well as further progress on local currency bond market development. In addition, capital flow volatility may call for an assessment of the macroprudential policy toolkit to help smoothen exposure to foreign currency debt and maturity mismatches.

Finally, structural policies should be aimed at further enhancing the diversification of EMEs in global trade and finance, boosting productivity and long-run growth potential and insulating economies from terms-of-trade shocks and spillovers from abroad. In this regard, improving efficiency in the management of public finances, as well as fostering more effective regulation and supervison in the financial sector, will help to bolster EME resilience during episodes of financial distress, including those driven by tightening global financial conditions.

References

Disyatat, Piti, and Gabriele Galati. 2007. "The Effectiveness of Foreign Exchange Intervention in Emerging Market Countries: Evidence from the Czech Koruna." *Journal of International Money and Finance* 26 (3): 383–402.

Hofmann, Boris, and Taejin Park. 2020. "The Broad Dollar Exchange Rate as an EME Risk Factor." *BIS Quarterly Review*. December 2020: 13–26.

International Monetary Fund. 2022. *Global Financial Stability Report: Navigating the High-Inflation Environment.* Washington, DC: International Monetary Fund.

Mohanty, Madhusudan S., and Bat-el Berger. 2013. "Central Bank Views on Foreign Exchange Intervention." BIS Paper No. 73.

The third risk is the longer-than-expected persistence of elevated inflation. Although inflation in major advanced economies and many regional economies has eased, it remains at an elevated level. There is uncertainty over how long elevated inflation will last; if longer than expected, it would reduce purchasing power and weaken asset values.

The fourth risk is uncertainty in the economic outlook in the region. Although fears of recession in major advanced economies have abated, external demand in many regional economies remains weak. There is also

uncertainty over how much the PRC's reopening will benefit other economies in the region.

Last but not least, higher interest rate levels may cause liquidity stress as the balance sheets of financial institutions and corporations weaken. Higher interest rate will lead to value losses in financial and real assets, while tightened financial conditions make refinancing difficult, putting pressure on high-leverage firms such as small banks and real estate companies. For example, during the review period, stress was observed in Viet Nam's corporate bond market, as many real estate firms found it hard to refinance their debt. This led to concerns over other firms' ability to repay debt obligations as liquidity in the market dries up. Similarly, the liquidity positions of banks with less diversified portfolios and large maturity

mismatches on their balance sheets must also be closely monitored to avoid the liquidity stress that led to bank failures such as Silicon Valley Bank. **Box 5** discusses the failure of Silicon Valley Bank and its implication for emerging East Asia.

Box 5: Implications of the Failure of Silicon Valley Bank for Emerging East Asia

Silicon Valley Bank (SVB) is a commercial bank specializing in providing lending and other services to technology companies in the startup phase.[a] At the end of 2022, SVB was the 16th largest bank in the United States (US) and the largest (in terms of deposits) in Silicon Valley. On 10 March, however, SVB's charter was revoked by the California Department of Financial Protection and Innovation, and the bank was placed under the receivership of the Federal Deposit Insurance Corporation.

Two key factors contributed to SVB's collapse. The first factor was a significant maturity mismatch in SVB's balance sheet. On the liability side, SVB's average total deposits saw rapid growth from 2019 to 2022, rising over three-fold from USD55.1 billion to USD185.8 billion (**Figure B5.1**).[b, c] By the end of 2022, average non-interest-bearing demand deposits had reached USD109.7 billion, accounting for 59% of average total deposits (footnote c). Meanwhile, during the pandemic, SVB was unable to expand its loan portfolio at a rate comparable to its deposit increases. Instead, SVB invested

most of its deposits in fixed-income securities such as mortgage-backed securities and US Treasuries. By the end of 2022, SVB held USD124.2 billion worth of available-for-sale and hold-to-maturity fixed-income securities, accounting for around 60% of its total interest-earning assets (**Figure B5.2**) (footnote c). These fixed-income securities bear a much longer maturity than demand deposits. Moreover, their market value declines as interest rates rise. This maturity mismatch can lead to liquidity risk when liquidity conditions tighten in the market.

The second factor was the lack of diversification that weakened SVB's liquidity position. SVB's client base is concentrated among startups and the technology sector. Amid a negative economic outlook, the bust in technology stocks, and slowing revenue growth, SVB's clients faced increased liquidity demands that led to large withdrawals.[d] In the fourth quarter of 2022, SVB reported a USD10.8 billion

Figure B5.1: Average Total Deposits of Silicon Valley Bank

USD billion

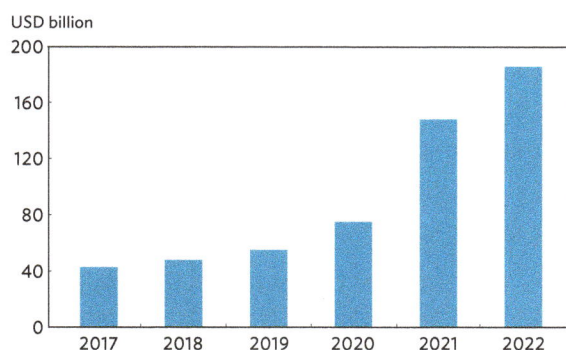

USD = United States dollar.
Source: SVB Financial Group annual reports.

Figure B5.2: Average Total Investment Securities versus Average Net Loans of Silicon Valley Bank

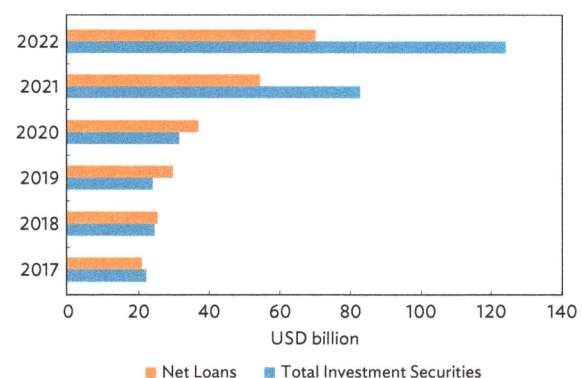

USD billion

■ Net Loans ■ Total Investment Securities

USD = United States dollar.
Source: SVB Financial Group annual reports.

---

[a] This box was written by Shu Tian (senior economist), Roselyn Regalado (financial analyst), and Russ Jason Lo (CFA, financial analyst) in the Economic Research and Regional Cooperation Department of the Asian Development Bank.
[b] United States Securities and Exchange Commission. 2021. *Annual Report for Silicon Valley Bank*. Washington, DC.
[c] United States Securities and Exchange Commission. 2022. *Annual Report for Silicon Valley Bank*. Washington, DC.
[d] The technology sector's subdued operational outlook is evidenced by the fact that several prominent IT companies were forced to conduct massive layoffs in late 2022 and early 2023. For example, in November 2022, Meta Platforms, the parent company of Facebook and Instagram, announced layoffs for 11,000 employees, equal to 13% of its workforce. In January 2023, Alphabet, the parent company of Google, laid off 12,000 employees, while Microsoft laid off 10,000 workers.

continued on next page

Box 5 *continued*

(5.8%) decrease in average on-balance sheet deposits compared to the previous quarter, as well as a USD10.0 billion decrease in off-balance sheet client investment funds.[e]

These two factors jointly exposed SVB to heightened interest rate and liquidity risks when the dimmed economic outlook combined with monetary policy tightening. As the US Federal Reserve aggressively raised interest rates to contain inflation, the debt securities held by SVB generated an unrealized mark-to-market loss of over USD15 billion at the end of 2022 for those held-to-maturity securities (footnote c). Facing rising liquidity pressure, SVB was forced to sell USD21 billion worth of security holdings on 8 March. This ill-timed securities sale realized a mark-to-market loss of USD1.8 billion and signaled the bank's liquidity stress. This triggered more liquidity demand among depositors, which quickly dried out the bank's liquidity. On 10 March, SVB was placed under receivership as regulators deemed the bank to be both insolvent and illiquid.

US regulators stepped in quickly to protect depositors and contain the impacts of this incident. To maintain confidence in the banking system and calm depositors' fears, US financial regulators announced emergency measures on 12 March. The Federal Reserve, jointly with the US Treasury and Federal Deposit Insurance Commission, announced that both insured and uninsured deposits would be safeguarded and depositors would be able to withdraw all of their funds starting on 13 March. In addition, the Federal Reserve said that it would launch a new facility, the Bank Term Funding Program, through which banks and other depository institutions would be able to secure loans of up to 1 year in maturity in exchange for eligible collateral such as US Treasuries, agency debt, and mortgage-backed securities.

The SVB incident will have financial stability implications for regulators in emerging East Asia. First, the liquidity positions of small banks with less diversified portfolios should be revisited to avoid similar incidents. In 2022, many regional central banks also raised interest rates aggressively to contain inflationary pressure. This led to value losses (either realized or unrealized) for both financial and real assets. Meanwhile, although emerging East Asia's economic outlook remains positive, growth in the region will moderate in 2023 amid weakened external demand. The region's small banks with less of a liquidity buffer could face similar liquidity stress when liquidity demand rises.

Second, the uncertainty that soured market sentiment could lead to contagion within US financial markets and around the world. Between 8 March and 13 March, the S&P 500 Index declined 3.4%; equity indexes in Germany and the United Kingdom fell 4.3% and 4.8%, respectively; and emerging East Asian equity markets fell 1.4%. Soured investment sentiment may further tighten liquidity conditions as investors become risk averse. This could translate into capital outflows from the region.

Meanwhile, another possible implication is that the SVB incident might slow the pace of monetary tightening in the US. According to the CME FedWatch, the probability of a 50 basis points rate hike at the Federal Open Market Committee's March meeting fell from 40.2% on 10 March to zero on 13 March, while the probability of there being no rate hike rose from zero to 24.7%. Last, but not least, some regional startups may be negatively affected by SVB's collapse if they have to seek alternative financial service providers. Given the dimmed economic outlook and soured investment sentiment, it might now be more difficult for startups to get funding.

---

[e] Silicon Valley Bank. 2023. SVB Financial Group Announces Fourth Quarter 2022 Financial Results. *News Release*. 19 January.

Bond Market Developments in the Fourth Quarter of 2022

Size and Composition

The local currency bond market in emerging East Asia reached a size of USD23.2 trillion at the end of December.

Emerging East Asia's local currency bond market (LCY) expanded at a slower pace in the fourth quarter (Q4) of 2022 than in the previous quarter (**Figure 1a**).[6] The region's LCY bond market totaled USD23.2 trillion at the end of December, with growth easing to 1.2% quarter-on-quarter (q-o-q) in Q4 2022 from 2.3% q-o-q in the third quarter (Q3). All markets except that of Viet Nam recorded a slowdown in growth in Q4 2022 compared with the previous quarter. Growth in government bonds outstanding in Q4 2022 was capped by a decline in issuance as most of the regions' governments had fulfilled their borrowing requirements earlier in the year. Meanwhile, corporate bond issuance contracted amid elevated borrowing costs due to monetary policy tightening by most of the region's central banks and bond default concerns in the People's Republic of China (PRC) and Viet Nam, particularly in the property sector in both economies.

Annual growth of outstanding LCY bonds in emerging East Asia moderated to 9.9% in Q4 2022 from 12.5% in the preceding quarter. All nine markets posted positive but weaker annual growth in Q4 2022 compared with Q3 2022 (**Figure 1b**). The markets of Viet Nam and the Philippines had the fastest year-on-year (y-o-y) growth rates in Q4 2022.

The LCY bond market of the PRC continued to be the largest in the region, reaching a size of USD18.5 trillion at the end of December. Its share of the region's LCY bond market was steady at 79.5% in both Q3 and Q4 2022. The PRC's LCY bond market growth eased to 1.3% q-o-q in Q4 2022 amid a slowdown in the government bond segment and a contraction in the corporate bond segment. The government continued to issue sovereign debt to finance stimulus measures and to roll over

Figure 1a: Growth of Select Emerging East Asian Local Currency Bond Markets in the Third and Fourth Quarters of 2022 (q-o-q, %)

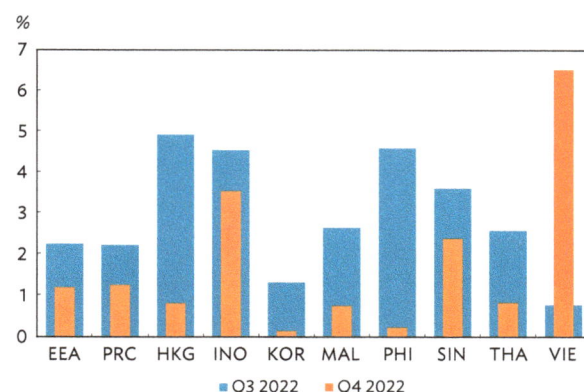

EEA = emerging East Asia; HKG = Hong Kong, China; INO = Indonesia; KOR = Republic of Korea; MAL = Malaysia; PHI = Philippines; PRC = People's Republic of China; q-o-q = quarter-on-quarter; Q3 = third quarter; Q4 = fourth quarter; SIN = Singapore; THA = Thailand; VIE = Viet Nam.

Notes:
1. For Singapore, corporate bonds outstanding are based on *AsianBondsOnline* estimates.
2. Growth rates are calculated from a local currency base and do not include currency effects.
3. Emerging East Asia growth figures are based on 31 December 2022 currency exchange rates and do not include currency effects.

Sources: People's Republic of China (CEIC Data Company); Hong Kong, China (Hong Kong Monetary Authority); Indonesia (Bank Indonesia; Directorate General of Budget Financing and Risk Management, Ministry of Finance; and Indonesia Stock Exchange); Republic of Korea (KG Zeroin Corporation and The Bank of Korea); Malaysia (Bank Negara Malaysia); Philippines (Bureau of the Treasury and Bloomberg LP); Singapore (Monetary Authority of Singapore and Bloomberg LP); Thailand (Bank of Thailand); and Viet Nam (Bloomberg LP and Vietnam Bond Market Association).

existing debt, albeit at a slower pace compared to prior quarters following the completion of local government bond quotas. Growth in government bonds in Q4 2022 stemmed from expansions in Treasury bonds and other government bonds (3.5% q-o-q), policy bank bonds (2.1% q-o-q), and local government bonds (1.1% q-o-q). On the other hand, the corporate bond market contracted 0.3% q-o-q, amid worsening property market debt distress.

The region's second-largest LCY bond market was that of the Republic of Korea, with an outstanding bond stock of USD2.3 trillion at the end of December. Its share of the

---

[6] Emerging East Asia is defined to include member states of the Association of Southeast Asian Nations (ASEAN) plus the People's Republic of China; Hong Kong, China; and the Republic of Korea.

Figure 1b: Growth of Select Emerging East Asian Local Currency Bond Markets in the Third and Fourth Quarters of 2022 (y-o-y, %)

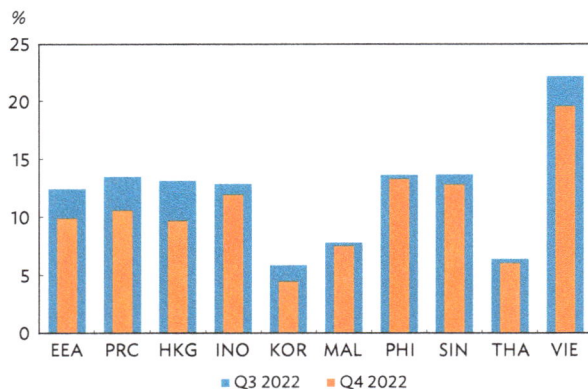

EEA = emerging East Asia; HKG = Hong Kong, China; INO = Indonesia; KOR = Republic of Korea; MAL = Malaysia; PHI = Philippines; PRC = People's Republic of China; Q3 = third quarter; Q4 = fourth quarter; SIN = Singapore; THA = Thailand; VIE = Viet Nam; y-o-y = year-on-year.

Notes:
1. For Singapore, corporate bonds outstanding are based on *AsianBondsOnline* estimates.
2. Growth rates are calculated from a local currency base and do not include currency effects.
3. Emerging East Asia growth figures are based on 31 December 2022 currency exchange rates and do not include currency effects.

Sources: People's Republic of China (CEIC Data Company); Hong Kong, China (Hong Kong Monetary Authority); Indonesia (Bank Indonesia; Directorate General of Budget Financing and Risk Management, Ministry of Finance; and Indonesia Stock Exchange); Republic of Korea (KG Zeroin Corporation and The Bank of Korea); Malaysia (Bank Negara Malaysia); Philippines (Bureau of the Treasury and Bloomberg LP); Singapore (Monetary Authority of Singapore and Bloomberg LP); Thailand (Bank of Thailand); and Viet Nam (Bloomberg LP and Vietnam Bond Market Association).

region's total outstanding LCY bonds stood at 10.1% at the end of Q4 2022. Overall growth in the Republic of Korea's LCY bonds was marginal at 0.1% q-o-q in Q4 2022 as the government bond segment contracted, while growth in the corporate bond segment eased. The government bond market contracted 0.3% q-o-q in Q4 2022, largely due to a high volume of maturities. The LCY corporate bond market inched up by only 0.4% q-o-q in Q4 2022 amid rising borrowing costs. To combat inflation, the Bank of Korea raised its policy rate by 50 basis points (bps) in October and 25 bps in November.

Hong Kong, China's LCY bond market reached a size of USD355.1 billion at the end of December, with overall growth moderating to 0.8% q-o-q and 9.7% y-o-y in Q4 2022. Growth eased for both the government and corporate bond segments. Quarterly expansion

in outstanding Exchange Fund Bills picked up, while the stock of Exchange Fund Notes continued to contract. Meanwhile, quarterly growth in outstanding Hong Kong Special Administrative Region bonds and corporate bonds moderated.

Total LCY bonds outstanding of the members of the Association of Southeast Asian Nations (ASEAN) reached USD2,058.4 billion at the end of December.[7] Overall growth in the region's LCY bond market dropped to 1.9% q-o-q in Q4 2022 from 3.3% q-o-q in the previous quarter, as all markets posted weaker q-o-q growth in Q4 2022 except for Viet Nam. ASEAN members' share of emerging East Asia's total LCY bond market inched up to 8.9% in Q4 2022 from 8.8% in Q3 2022. The LCY bond markets of Singapore and Thailand were the region's largest, while Viet Nam remained the region's smallest.

Singapore's LCY bond stock totaled USD494.0 billion at the end of December, with growth moderating to 2.4% q-o-q in Q4 2022 from 3.6% q-o-q in the previous quarter. This was primarily driven by slower growth in the government bond segment as expansions in Singapore Government Securities and Monetary Authority of Singapore bills moderated. Meanwhile, the LCY corporate bond market expanded 1.2% q-o-q in Q4 2022, after a nominal contraction in Q3 2022.

Thailand's LCY bond market reached a size of USD451.5 billion at the end of December after rising a marginal 0.8% q-o-q in Q4 2022 due to weaker expansions in both the government and corporate bond segments. Government bonds and Treasury bills, as well as state-owned enterprise bonds and other bonds, posted weaker growth in Q4 2022 than in the previous quarter, while the stock of Bank of Thailand bonds continued to contract. The Government of Thailand issued THB30.0 billion (USD0.9 billion) of sustainability bonds in December. Meanwhile, growth in the LCY corporate bond market eased to 1.4% q-o-q in Q4 2022 from 3.4% q-o-q in the previous quarter.

Malaysia's LCY bond stock totaled USD423.9 billion at the end of December, with growth moderating to 0.8% q-o-q in Q4 2022 from 2.6% q-o-q in the preceding quarter. The weaker growth was due to a slowdown in

---

[7] LCY bond statistics for ASEAN include the markets of Indonesia, Malaysia, the Philippines, Singapore, Thailand, and Viet Nam.

both the government and corporate bond segments. Growth in government bonds stemmed primarily from central government bonds, which comprised 99.0% of total government bonds at the end of December.

Malaysia's *sukuk* (Islamic bond) market, which is the largest in emerging East Asia, totaled USD268.4 billion at the end of December. Government *sukuk* amounted to USD114.2 billion, comprising 47.8% of the total LCY government bond market. Corporate *sukuk* totaled USD154.2 billion, representing 83.3% of Malaysia's LCY corporate bond market.

The LCY bond market of Indonesia reached a size of USD382.2 billion at the end of December, with overall growth decelerating to 3.5% q-o-q in Q4 2022 from 4.5% q-o-q in Q3 2022. Growth in central government bonds, which account for the largest share of government bonds, eased to 4.1% q-o-q in Q4 2022 from 5.2% q-o-q in Q3 2022 on reduced issuance as the government had fulfilled most of its financing requirements in earlier quarters. The corporate bond market contracted 2.7% q-o-q, largely due to rising borrowing costs as Bank Indonesia hiked its policy rate—in October, November, and December by a total of 125 bps—to temper inflation.

Indonesia's *sukuk* market totaled USD68.4 billion at the end of December, on growth of 3.0% q-o-q. *Sukuk* outstanding represented 18.6% of Indonesia's LCY bond market. Government *sukuk* totaled USD68.4 billion at the end of December, comprising 19.3% of the LCY government bond market. Corporate *sukuk* amounted to USD2.7 billion, representing 9.4% of the LCY corporate bond market.

At the end of December, the Philippines' outstanding LCY bond stock totaled USD200.9 billion, with growth decelerating to 0.2% q-o-q in Q4 2022, driven by a contraction in the government bond segment coupled with a weaker expansion in the corporate bond segment. Government bonds outstanding declined 0.4% q-o-q in Q4 2022, due primarily to a large volume of maturities in Treasury bills and other government bonds. Meanwhile, growth in corporate bonds outstanding moderated to 4.4% q-o-q in Q4 2022 on continued policy rate hikes by the Bangko Sentral ng Pilipinas (BSP) to address persistent inflation.

Viet Nam's LCY bond market remained the smallest in emerging East Asia, with an outstanding bond stock of USD105.7 billion at the end of December. Growth in Viet Nam's LCY bond market accelerated to 6.5% q-o-q in Q4 2022 from 0.8% q-o-q in the previous quarter, driven primarily by a rebound in the government bond segment. The stock of LCY government bonds jumped 9.9% q-o-q in Q4 2022, reversing a 1.7% q-o-q contraction in the previous quarter. Expansions in Treasury bonds, State Bank of Vietnam bills, and government-guaranteed and municipal bonds supported growth in the government bond segment. Meanwhile, the corporate bond market posted a 0.9% q-o-q decline in Q4 2022 amid a credit crunch. In September, the Government of Viet Nam issued Decree 65, tightening regulation on the offering and trading of privately issued bonds. As a majority of corporate bonds in Viet Nam are issued via private placement, Decree 65 capped issuance of bonds, leading to a decline in the corporate bond stock during the quarter. Issuers faced difficulties in issuing bonds or refinancing maturing obligations, as government investigations in the corporate bond market raised concerns over high-risk issuers, particularly in the real estate sector. The spillover of negative sentiment affected other sectors, tightening funding channels even for investment grade issuers.

Emerging East Asia's LCY bond market continued to be dominated by government bonds. The region's aggregate LCY government bond stock totaled USD14.8 trillion at the end of December, accounting for 63.9% of the region's total LCY bond stock (**Table 1**). Growth in the region's government bonds eased to 1.9% q-o-q in Q4 2022 from 2.8% q-o-q in Q3 2022. Except for the Philippines and the Republic of Korea, all of the region's LCY government bond markets posted positive q-o-q growth in Q4 2022.

With outstanding LCY government bonds amounting to USD12.1 trillion, the PRC's government bond market remained the largest in the region, comprising 81.8% of the region's LCY government bond stock at the end of Q4 2022. The Republic of Korea's LCY government bond market was the region's second-largest government bond market at USD1.0 trillion. ASEAN economies' aggregate LCY government bonds totaled USD1.5 trillion at the end of December, representing 10.3% of emerging East Asia's total LCY government bond market. Among ASEAN economies, Singapore had the largest government bond market, while Viet Nam had the smallest.

Table 1: Size and Composition of Select Emerging East Asian Local Currency Bond Markets

| | Q4 2021 | | Q3 2022 | | Q4 2022 | | Growth Rate (LCY-base %) | | | | Growth Rate (USD-base %) | | | |
| | Amount (USD billion) | % share | Amount (USD billion) | % share | Amount (USD billion) | % share | Q4 2021 | | Q4 2022 | | Q4 2021 | | Q4 2022 | |
							q-o-q	y-o-y	q-o-q	y-o-y	q-o-q	y-o-y	q-o-q	y-o-y
China, People's Rep. of														
Total	18,117	100.0	17,676	100.0	18,463	100.0	3.9	13.6	1.3	10.6	5.4	16.6	4.5	1.9
Government	11,701	64.6	11,512	65.1	12,125	65.7	4.5	14.2	2.1	12.5	6.0	17.3	5.3	3.6
Corporate	6,416	35.4	6,164	34.9	6,338	34.3	2.9	12.4	(0.3)	7.2	4.4	15.4	2.8	(1.2)
Hong Kong, China														
Total	324	100.0	350	100.0	355	100.0	4.0	5.0	0.8	9.7	3.8	4.4	1.4	9.7
Government	169	52.2	183	52.1	185	52.2	5.2	11.2	0.9	9.8	5.0	10.5	1.6	9.7
Corporate	155	47.8	168	47.9	170	47.8	2.7	(1.0)	0.7	9.6	2.6	(1.5)	1.3	9.5
Indonesia														
Total	373	100.0	377	100.0	382	100.0	4.4	17.7	3.5	12.0	4.9	16.0	1.3	2.5
Government	343	91.9	347	92.0	354	92.5	4.6	19.4	4.1	12.7	5.1	17.7	1.8	3.2
Corporate	30	8.1	30	8.0	29	7.5	2.0	1.1	(2.7)	3.5	2.4	(0.4)	(4.8)	(5.3)
Korea, Rep. of														
Total	2,390	100.0	2,071	100.0	2,346	100.0	1.5	7.9	0.1	4.5	1.1	(1.4)	13.2	(1.9)
Government	995	41.6	883	42.6	996	42.5	0.2	9.6	(0.3)	6.6	(0.2)	0.1	12.8	0.1
Corporate	1,396	58.4	1,188	57.4	1,350	57.5	2.4	6.8	0.4	2.9	2.0	(2.4)	13.6	(3.3)
Malaysia														
Total	417	100.0	400	100.0	424	100.0	1.0	8.2	0.8	7.5	1.5	4.4	6.1	1.7
Government	228	54.7	226	56.6	239	56.3	1.2	11.4	0.2	10.7	1.7	7.5	5.5	4.7
Corporate	189	45.3	173	43.4	185	43.7	0.8	4.6	1.4	3.7	1.3	1.0	6.8	(1.9)
Philippines														
Total	194	100.0	190	100.0	201	100.0	0.5	14.8	0.2	13.3	0.5	8.2	5.5	3.7
Government	164	84.7	164	86.3	172	85.7	0.5	20.3	(0.4)	14.7	0.5	13.3	4.8	4.9
Corporate	30	15.3	26	13.7	29	14.3	0.6	(8.1)	4.4	5.8	0.6	(13.4)	9.9	(3.2)
Singapore														
Total	435	100.0	450	100.0	494	100.0	3.2	17.9	2.4	12.8	3.8	15.5	9.7	13.6
Government	305	70.2	327	72.6	360	72.9	4.1	24.9	2.9	17.2	4.8	22.4	10.2	18.1
Corporate	130	29.8	124	27.4	134	27.1	1.0	4.2	1.2	2.5	1.7	2.1	8.4	3.2
Thailand														
Total	441	100.0	411	100.0	452	100.0	1.1	5.8	0.8	6.1	44.0	58.7	9.9	2.4
Government	321	72.8	294	71.7	323	71.5	1.6	4.7	0.6	4.2	41.9	54.2	9.7	0.6
Corporate	120	27.2	116	28.3	129	28.5	0.01	8.6	1.4	11.0	49.7	71.9	10.6	7.2
Viet Nam														
Total	92	100.0	98	100.0	106	100.0	8.8	25.5	6.5	19.6	8.5	27.0	7.5	15.5
Government	65	71.3	67	68.6	75	70.8	4.3	8.0	9.9	18.7	4.0	9.3	11.0	14.7
Corporate	26	28.7	31	31.4	31	29.2	21.9	110.0	(0.9)	21.8	21.6	112.5	0.04	17.6
Emerging East Asia														
Total	22,782	100.0	22,024	100.0	23,222	100.0	3.5	12.7	1.2	9.9	5.3	14.5	5.4	1.9
Government	14,290	62.7	14,004	63.6	14,828	63.9	4.0	13.9	1.9	12.0	5.9	16.3	5.9	3.8
Corporate	8,492	37.3	8,020	36.4	8,394	36.1	2.8	10.8	(0.08)	6.5	4.3	11.6	4.7	(1.2)
Japan														
Total	11,338	100.0	9,084	100.0	10,154	100.0	2.6	4.3	1.3	2.0	(0.8)	(6.4)	11.8	(10.4)
Government	10,515	92.7	8,417	92.7	9,406	92.6	2.6	4.2	1.2	1.9	(0.8)	(6.5)	11.7	(10.5)
Corporate	823	7.3	667	7.3	748	7.4	2.9	6.0	1.7	3.5	(0.5)	(4.9)	12.2	(9.1)

( ) = negative, LCY = local currency, q-o-q = quarter-on-quarter, Q3 = third quarter, Q4 = fourth quarter, USD = United States dollar, y-o-y = year-on-year.

Notes:
1. For Singapore, corporate bonds outstanding are based on *AsianBondsOnline* estimates.
2. Corporate bonds include issues by financial institutions.
3. Bloomberg LP end-of-period LCY–USD rates are used.
4. For LCY base, emerging East Asia growth figures are based on 31 December 2022 currency exchange rates and do not include currency effects.

Sources: People's Republic of China (CEIC Data Company); Hong Kong, China (Hong Kong Monetary Authority); Indonesia (Bank Indonesia; Directorate General of Budget Financing and Risk Management, Ministry of Finance; and Indonesia Stock Exchange); Republic of Korea (KG Zeroin Corporation and The Bank of Korea); Malaysia (Bank Negara Malaysia); Philippines (Bureau of the Treasury and Bloomberg LP); Singapore (Monetary Authority of Singapore and Bloomberg LP); Thailand (Bank of Thailand); Viet Nam (Bloomberg LP and Vietnam Bond Market Association); and Japan (Japan Securities Dealers Association).

Emerging East Asia's LCY government bond stock remained concentrated in medium- to long-term tenors (**Figure 2**). Government bonds with maturities longer than 5 years comprised 54.4% of the region's total government bond market at the end of Q4 2022, and the size-weighted tenor of outstanding LCY government bonds in the region was 9.1 years. In nearly all markets, at least half of government bonds had maturities longer than 5 years. The exceptions were Hong Kong, China, where 75.4% of government bonds had tenors of 1–3 years, due to strong market demand for short-term securities, and the Philippines, where 53.6% of government bonds had maturities of up to 5 years. Governments like Thailand, which have extended debt repayment period through bond switch operations, had government bond maturity profiles concentrated in longer tenors.

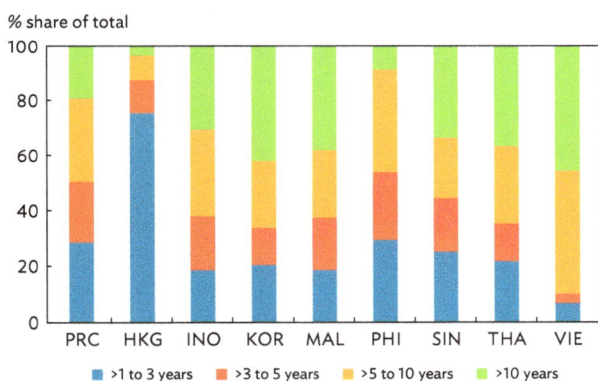

Figure 2: Maturity Structure of Local Currency Government Bonds Outstanding in Select Emerging East Asian Markets

% share of total

HKG = Hong Kong, China; INO = Indonesia; KOR = Korea, Rep. of; MAL = Malaysia; PHI = Philippines; PRC = China, People's Rep. of; SIN = Singapore; THA = Thailand; VIE = Viet Nam.

Notes:
1. Government bonds include Treasury bills and bonds.
2. Data as of 31 December 2022.

Sources: People's Republic of China (Bloomberg LP); Hong Kong, China (Hong Kong Monetary Authority); Indonesia (Directorate General of Budget Financing and Risk Management, Ministry of Finance); Republic of Korea (Bloomberg LP); Malaysia (Bank Negara Malaysia Fully Automated System for Issuing/Tendering); Philippines (Bureau of the Treasury); Singapore (Monetary Authority of Singapore); Thailand (Bank of Thailand); and Viet Nam (Bloomberg LP).

The LCY corporate bond market in emerging East Asia reached a size of USD8.4 trillion at the end of December, comprising 36.1% of the region's LCY bond stock. Emerging East Asia's LCY corporate bond market contracted 0.1% q-o-q in Q4 2022, reversing the 1.3% q-o-q expansion posted in the previous quarter. The contraction in the PRC's corporate bond market— the region's largest—drove the overall decline in the

region's corporate bond stock. In addition, the corporate bond markets of Indonesia and Viet Nam also recorded quarterly contractions in Q4 2022. The rest of the region's corporate bond markets except for Singapore experienced weaker growth in Q4 2022 than in the prior quarter.

The combined shares of the PRC and the Republic of Korea represented over 90.0% of the region's corporate bond market at the end of December. ASEAN member economies' aggregate corporate bond stock comprised 6.4% of the region's total corporate bond market. Within ASEAN, Malaysia had the largest corporate bond market at the end of December, while Indonesia and the Philippines were home to the smallest corporate bond market in the region.

The ratio of emerging East Asia's bond market to the region's gross domestic product (GDP) slightly rose to 101.7% in Q4 2022 from 101.0% in Q3 2022 (**Figure 3**), as the outstanding size of all bond markets in the region posted q-o-q increases. In addition, the 5.4% q-o-q increase in the regional bond market's size (in United States dollar terms) was higher than the region's GDP growth rate of 4.7% q-o-q. The region's government bond market as a share of GDP rose to 64.9% in Q4 2022 from 64.2% in Q3 2022, while that of the region's corporate bond market was almost at par with the previous quarter at 36.8%.

Five out of nine economies in the region posted higher total bonds to GDP shares in Q4 2022 than the previous quarter. The bond markets that posted lower ratios include the Republic of Korea, Malaysia, the Philippines, and Thailand, as their q-o-q GDP growth rates were higher than the quarterly increases in their respective bond markets. The Republic of Korea continued to have the highest share at 151.1%, followed by Malaysia and the PRC at 123.9% and 105.2%, respectively. In terms of q-o-q percentage points increase, Hong Kong, China posted the largest uptick of 1.3, followed by Singapore and Viet Nam with 0.9 each. Meanwhile, Indonesia (30.4%) and Viet Nam (26.3%) had the lowest bonds-to-GDP ratios in the region.

In Q4 2022, Singapore had the highest government bonds-to-GDP share at 75.0%, followed by Malaysia at 69.7% and the PRC at 69.1%, while Viet Nam had the lowest share at 18.6%. As for the corporate bond segment, the Republic of Korea (86.9%) and Malaysia (54.1%) had the highest shares, while Indonesia had the smallest share at 2.3%.

Figure 3: Size and Composition of Select Emerging East Asian Local Currency Bond Markets (share of GDP)

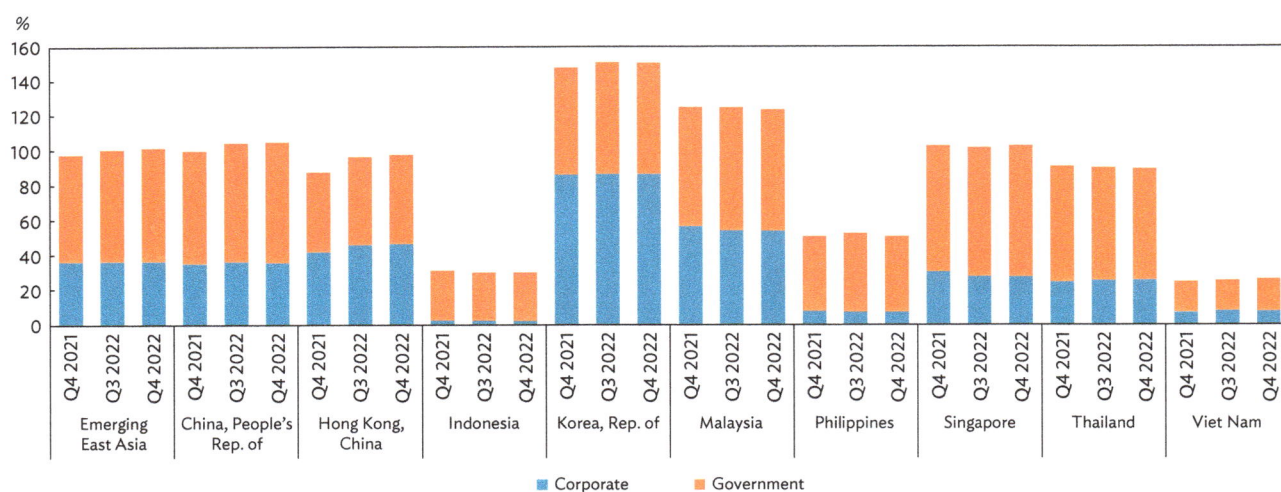

GDP = gross domestic product, Q3 = third quarter, Q4 = fourth quarter.
Notes:
1. Data for GDP is from CEIC.
2. For Singapore, corporate bonds outstanding are based on *AsianBondsOnline* estimates.
Sources: People's Republic of China (CEIC Data Company); Hong Kong, China (Hong Kong Monetary Authority); Indonesia (Bank Indonesia; Directorate General of Budget Financing and Risk Management, Ministry of Finance; and Indonesia Stock Exchange); Republic of Korea (KG Zeroin Corporation and The Bank of Korea); Malaysia (Bank Negara Malaysia); Philippines (Bureau of the Treasury and Bloomberg LP); Singapore (Monetary Authority of Singapore and Bloomberg LP); Thailand (Bank of Thailand); and Viet Nam (Bloomberg LP and Vietnam Bond Market Association).

Foreign Bond Flows

Emerging East Asia posted net foreign inflows of USD1.9 billion in Q4 2022 as market sentiment improved.

The region posted net foreign inflows of USD1.9 billion in Q4 2022, a reversal from the USD5.6 billion of net outflows in the previous quarter. This was largely driven by net inflows in November and December. October registered net outflows of USD3.8 billion due to expectations that the Federal Reserve would maintain its aggressive monetary tightening as September US inflation was still higher than expected. Nearly all markets posted outflows during the month led by Indonesia and Malaysia.

Global risk sentiment started to shift in November following the Federal Reserve's 1–2 November monetary policy meeting at which the possibility of the start in a slowdown in the pace of its rate hikes was indicated. This resulted in USD2.2 billion of net foreign inflows into the region's LCY government bond markets, largely driven by Indonesia and Thailand. In December, net foreign inflows to the region rose to USD3.5 billion following a smaller rate hike of 50 bps from the Federal Reserve at

its 13–14 December monetary policy meeting, following a series of 75 bps hikes. Nearly all regional markets, led by the PRC, posted net inflows during the month. The easing of the "zero COVID" policy in the PRC and increased expectations of its reopening resulted in inflows into its government bond market. Moreover, this also drove inflows to other markets in the region due to their trade linkages with the PRC, providing support to regional economic growth. The only markets that registered outflows in December were the Republic of Korea, which was mostly due to a large volume of maturities, and Malaysia. In January, the region posted net foreign outflows of USD1.8 billion, largely driven by the USD5.3 billion of net outflows from the Republic of Korea. If excluding the Republic of Korea, net foreign inflows amounted to USD3.6 billion as foreign demand for the region's government bonds picked up in Q4 2022.

Thailand posted the largest quarterly net foreign inflows in the region in Q4 2022 at USD3.2 billion. This was driven by net inflows of USD2.1 billion and USD1.6 billion in November and December, respectively, largely offsetting the USD0.5 billion of outflows in October. Increased optimism on the reopening of the PRC, which is expected to result to increased trade and a boost to Thailand's tourism industry, drove the surge in foreign flows into the domestic bond market. In January, domestic bonds continued to register net foreign inflows, albeit at a lower volume of USD0.9 billion.

In Q4 2022, Indonesia posted its first quarterly net inflows for the year at USD2.1 billion, reversing net outflows of USD3.3 billion in the previous quarter. High domestic bond yields drove the USD1.6 billion and USD1.7 billion of net inflows in November and December, respectively, which offset the USD1.1 billion of net foreign outflows in October. Following a shift from its accommodative stance starting in August, Bank Indonesia continued with its monetary policy tightening in Q4 2022, delivering a total of 125 bps of rate hikes. Net foreign inflows rose further to USD3.3 billion in January 2023.

In the PRC, foreign investors continued to sell domestic government bonds in October and November, resulting in monthly net outflows of USD0.8 billion and USD2.2 billion, respectively (**Figure 4**). However, this shifted following announcements in mid-November that the government would ease its zero COVID policy

Figure 4: Foreign Capital Flows in Select Emerging East Asian Local Currency Bond Markets

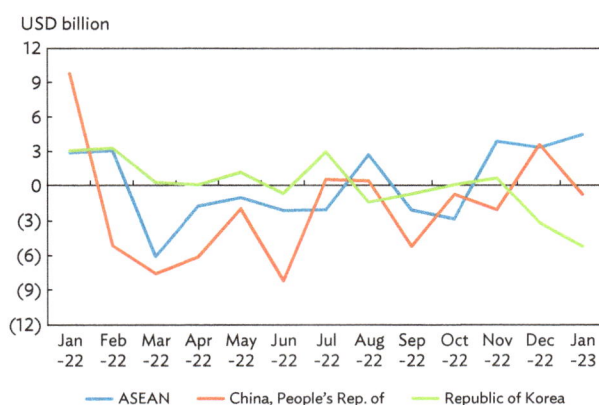

( ) = negative, ASEAN = Association of Southeast Asian Nations, USD = United States dollar.

Notes:
1. The Republic of Korea and Thailand provided data on bond flows. For the People's Republic of China, Indonesia, Malaysia, and the Philippines, month-on-month changes in foreign holdings of local currency government bonds were used as a proxy for bond flows.
2. Data are as of 31 January 2023.
3. Figures were computed based on 31 January 2023 exchange rates and do not include currency effects.

Sources: People's Republic of China (Bloomberg LP); Indonesia (Directorate General of Budget Financing and Risk Management, Ministry of Finance); Republic of Korea (Financial Supervisory Service); Malaysia (Bank Negara Malaysia); Philippines (Bureau of the Treasury); and Thailand (Thai Bond Market Association).

and on increased expectations of its reopening. Rising domestic bond yields, narrowing negative interest rate differentials with US Treasuries, and the appreciation of the Chinese yuan together resulted in net inflows of USD3.5 billion in December. However, foreign buying reversed in January, with the PRC incurring USD0.8 billion of net foreign outflows. Investors anticipated the pace of the economy's reopening and the government's continued loose monetary policy, and domestic bond yields remained low relative to US Treasuries.

In the Republic of Korea, foreign demand remained muted in Q4 2022 due to the continued narrowing of interest rate differentials with US Treasuries in October, and as US Treasury yields surpassed domestic bond yields starting in November. The Bank of Korea continued its monetary policy tightening during the quarter but at a much slower pace compared to the Federal Reserve. The Bank of Korea is also projected to slow its rate hikes due to rising domestic credit market risks and expectations of a domestic economic slowdown. This resulted in marginal net inflows of USD0.01 billion and USD0.6 billion in October and November, respectively. In December, the Republic of Korea's LCY government bond market registered net outflows of USD3.3 billion. Aggregate net foreign outflows in Q4 2022 amounted to USD2.7 billion due to large maturities and expectations that January would be the end of the Bank of Korea's tightening cycle. In January, net outflows increased further to USD5.3 billion as foreign investors continued to offload domestic bonds, particularly those with tenors of less than 1 year. This was due to the continued decline in bond yields vis-à-vis rising US yields and market expectations of a possible rate cut this year in the Republic of Korea.

In Malaysia, foreign investors continued to sell domestic government bonds, posting quarterly net outflows of USD1.9 billion in Q4 2022. As with the rest in the region, Malaysia incurred USD1.5 billion of outflows in October due to rising US Treasury yields. Bank Negara Malaysia only raised policy rates once during the quarter, by 25 bps in its November monetary policy meeting, which was much slower than the Federal Reserve's tightening. However, net foreign outflows declined toward the end of the year to USD0.3 billion and USD0.2 billion in November and December, respectively, on the Federal Reserve's less hawkish stance at its November monetary policy meeting. In January, Malaysia posted its first monthly net foreign inflows since August at USD0.1 bilion.

Figure 5: Investor Profiles of Local Currency Government Bonds in Select Emerging East Asian Markets

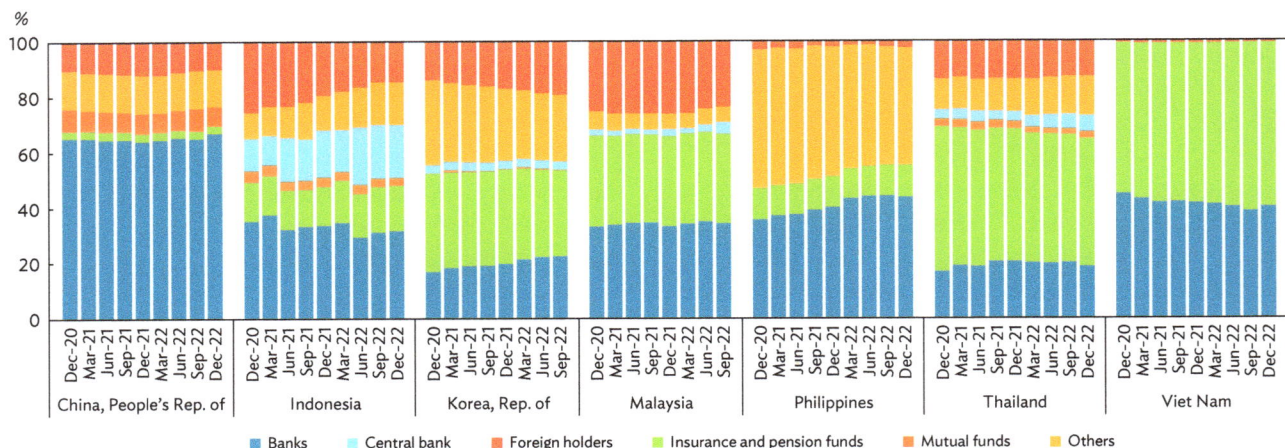

Notes:
1. Data for the Republic of Korea and Malaysia are up to September 2022.
2. "Others" include government institutions, individuals, securities companies, custodians, private corporations, and all other investors not elsewhere classified.

Sources: People's Republic of China (CEIC Data Company); Indonesia (Directorate General of Budget Financing and Risk Management, Ministry of Finance); Republic of Korea (The Bank of Korea); Malaysia (Bank Negara Malaysia); Philippines (Bureau of the Treasury); Thailand (Bank of Thailand); and Viet Nam (Ministry of Finance).

The Philippines continued to post monthly net inflows during Q4 2022 with a quarterly aggregate amount of USD0.7 billion. This was largely driven by high domestic bond yields as the BSP continued to hike rates during the quarter. The Philippines continued to register net foreign inflows in January of USD0.1 billion.

At the end of December, banks and insurance and pension funds remained the largest investor groups in most LCY government bond markets in the region (**Figure 5**). Their shares also increased in Q4 2022 as foreign ownership of government bonds slightly declined during the quarter. Central banks also saw increases in their participation in the bond market, particularly in Indonesia and Thailand.

Local Currency Bond Issuance

Aggregate issuance of local currency bonds by emerging East Asian economies reached a record-high volume in 2022.

Regional LCY bond sales in emerging East Asia remained robust in 2022, posting record-high volume. Total issuance in the region tallied USD9.0 trillion, up 6.8% y-o-y from the USD8.4 trillion recorded in 2021. Quarterly issuance volumes remained above the USD2.0 trillion mark for the seventh consecutive quarter amid monetary tightening in most regional economies in 2022 (**Figure 6**).

Figure 6: Local Currency Bond Issuance in Select Emerging East Asian Markets

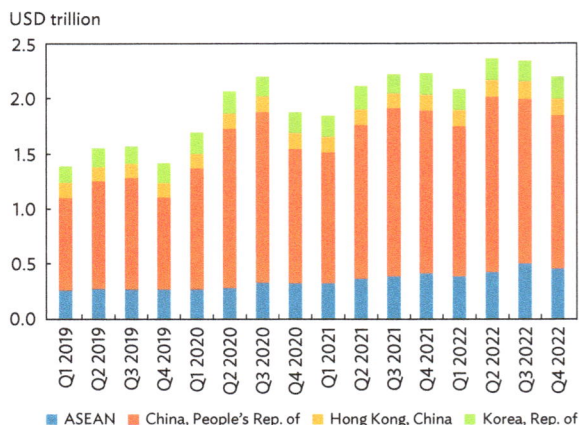

ASEAN = Association of Southeast Asian Nations, Q1 = first quarter, Q2 = second quarter, Q3 = third quarter, Q4 = fourth quarter, USD = United States dollar.

Notes:
1. ASEAN comprises the markets of Indonesia, Malaysia, the Philippines, Singapore, Thailand, and Viet Nam.
2. Figures were computed based on 31 December 2022 currency exchange rates and do not include currency effects.

Sources: People's Republic of China (CEIC Data Company); Hong Kong, China (Hong Kong Monetary Authority); Indonesia (Bank Indonesia; Directorate General of Budget Financing and Risk Management, Ministry of Finance; and Indonesia Stock Exchange); Republic of Korea (KG Zeroin Corporation and The Bank of Korea); Malaysia (Bank Negara Malaysia); Philippines (Bureau of the Treasury and Bloomberg LP); Singapore (Monetary Authority of Singapore and Bloomberg LP); Thailand (Bank of Thailand); and Viet Nam (Bloomberg LP, Hanoi Stock Exchange, and Vietnam Bond Market Association).

In Q4 2022, new bond sales reached USD2.2 trillion, contracting on both a q-o-q and y-o-y basis. The decline in regional bond issuance accelerated to 6.7% q-o-q in Q4 2022 from 1.0% q-o-q in Q3 2022, with all bond segments posting contractions. On a y-o-y basis, issuance fell 1.9% in Q4 2022 after rising 5.6% in the earlier quarter, due mainly to less issuance by corporates. The decline in issuance volume was largely influenced by rising borrowing costs and markets having completed their bond issuance targets earlier than planned.

Across different bond types, Treasury and other government bonds accounted for the largest share of the region's aggregate issuance volume in Q4 2022 (**Figure 7**). The share of Treasury and other government bonds to total issuance, however, slipped to 40.9% in Q4 2022 from 42.2% in Q3 2022, but was still higher than Q4 2021's 38.0%. All emerging East Asian economies issued a lower volume of Treasury and other government bonds during the quarter, as most economies had already fulfilled their borrowing plans, with Thailand and Viet Nam as the exception. Treasury and other government bonds contracted the most among bond types, declining 9.5% q-o-q but rising 5.6% y-o-y in Q4 2022.

In Q4 2022, Treasury instruments issued in most markets in emerging East Asia were dominated by medium- to long-term maturities. The size-weighted tenor of LCY government bond issuance during the quarter was 5.9 years, with 60.4% of total Treasury bonds issued in Q4 2022 having a tenor of more than 5 years. This was broadly similar with the 60.6% share in Q3 2022 but was up from 55.4% in Q4 2021 (**Figure 8**). Issuance of Treasury bonds with maturities of 5 years or less accounted for 39.6% of the issuance total during Q4 2022.

Central bank bond issuance during the quarter declined 5.6% q-o-q in Q4 2022, as most central banks in the region opted to raise policy rates to combat inflationary pressure. Most regional central banks had less issuance of bonds during the quarter compared with Q3 2022, with the Hong Kong Monetary Authority and the Bank of Thailand as the exceptions. Bonds issued by the region's central banks reached USD479.8 billion, with their aggregate share of the regional issuance total inching up to 22.0% in Q4 2022 from 21.7% in the prior quarter.

Amid the tightening monetary stances of most central banks in emerging East Asia, rising borrowing costs dragged down corporate bond issuance during the quarter. New issuance of corporate bonds reached USD810.4 billion in Q4 2022 on contractions of 4.0% q-o-q and 15.0% y-o-y. Six out of the nine regional economies saw contractions in their issuance of corporate bonds during the quarter. The only markets that recorded q-o-q increases were those of the Republic of Korea, Malaysia, and the Philippines. The share of corporate bonds in the issuance total inched up to 37.1% in Q4 2022 from 36.1% in the prior quarter.

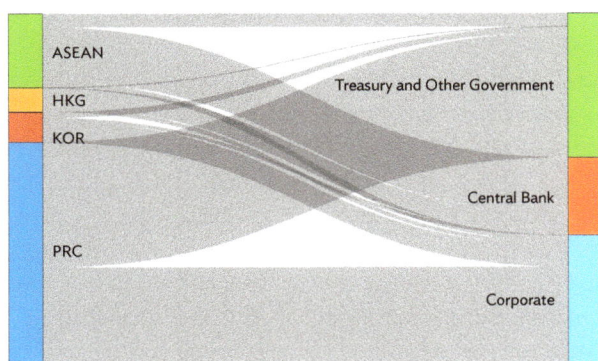

Figure 7: Local Currency Bond Issuance in the Fourth Quarter of 2022 by Economy and Type of Bond

ASEAN = Association of Southeast Asian Nations; HKG = Hong Kong, China; KOR = Republic of Korea; PRC = People's Republic of China.
Source: *AsianBondsOnline*.

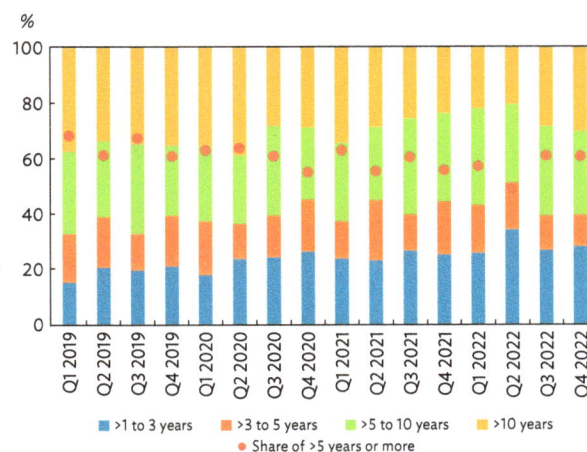

Figure 8: Maturity Structure of Quarterly Local Currency Government Bond Issuance in Select Emerging East Asian Markets

Q1 = first quarter, Q2 = second quarter, Q3 = third quarter, Q4 = fourth quarter.
Note: Figures were computed based on 31 December 2022 currency exchange rates and do not include currency effects.
Source: *AsianBondsOnline* computations based on various local sources.

In Q4 2022, seven out of the nine emerging East Asian economies tapered their respective issuance volumes compared with Q3 2022 (**Table 2**). On a q-o-q basis, the only markets that saw increased issuance of LCY bonds were those of the Republic of Korea and Malaysia. Relative to the same period a year earlier, overall issuance rose in Hong Kong, China; Malaysia; the Philippines; Singapore; and Thailand.

In the PRC, LCY bond issuance continued to decline, falling 6.7% q-o-q as total issuance reached USD1.4 trillion in Q4 2022 after shrinking 5.9% q-o-q in Q3 2022. Government bond sales fell, led primarily by a drop in local government bond issuance. Local government bond issuance declined 9.9% q-o-q in Q4 2022 as many local governments had fully utilized their special bond quotas by the end of June. The decline was offset by a 7.5% q-o-q gain in Treasury bonds as the PRC continued to provide fiscal stimulus to support the economy. In December, the Government of the PRC issued CNY750 billion worth of special bonds to finance economic and social development. Corporate bond issuance in the PRC also contracted 6.5% q-o-q in Q4 2022, as companies were concerned about the PRC's economic prospects.

In the Republic of Korea, bond issuance inched up 0.3% q-o-q to USD186.7 billion in Q4 2022 after a 5.0% q-o-q decline in the previous quarter. The reduced government bond issuance dragged down the Republic of Korea's bond issuance total in Q4 2022, following the frontloading policy that the government pursued in the first half of the year. Central bank bond issuance also contributed to the decline in government bond issuance, falling 8.2% q-o-q as the Bank of Korea scaled back its money market operations. However, corporate bond market sentiment improved, with corporate bond issuance extending its growth to 12.4% q-o-q in Q4 2022.

New bonds issued in Hong Kong, China reached USD149.9 billion in Q4 2022, representing a contraction of 6.7% q-o-q. The decline was largely contributed by reduced issuance of Treasury and other government bonds during the quarter, which followed from a high base in Q3 2022 due to an issuance of Silver Bonds. In addition, corporate bond issuance declined amid rising borrowing costs. Interest rate adjustments in the US and Hong Kong, China are largely aligned.

Aggregate LCY bond sales of ASEAN member markets tallied USD456.4 billion in Q4 2022, a contraction of 9.3% q-o-q after posting strong growth of 18.0% q-o-q in the preceding quarter. In the same period, issuance growth also moderated to 10.0% y-o-y from 30.1% y-o-y. Among ASEAN markets, only Malaysia had an overall increase in issuance during the quarter in review. Within ASEAN, the largest issuer was Singapore, which accounted for a 61.2% share of the ASEAN issuance total. Next was Thailand with a 14.0% share, followed by Indonesia and the Philippines each having an 8.5% share.

Singapore remained the most active issuer of LCY bonds among ASEAN peers in Q4 2022, despite issuance contracting across all bond types on a q-o-q basis. Government bond issuance, which largely comprised 99.3% of the total issuance volume, sank 2.7% q-o-q in Q4 2022. Corporate bond issuance declined a much faster 31.9% q-o-q; however, its share of the overall issuance tally was negligible.

Bond issuance activities marginally slowed in Thailand, dragged down by weak sales in the corporate bond segment. Overall issuance slipped 0.3% q-o-q in Q4 2022 amid rising borrowing costs that restrained corporate bond issuance. In contrast, issuance by the government, particularly for Treasury and other government bonds, climbed during the quarter following the start of a new fiscal year in October. The government, however, aims to cut its borrowings in fiscal year 2022–2023 as it scales back on coronavirus disease (COVID-19) related spending.

LCY bond sales in Indonesia totaled USD38.8 billion in Q4 2022, with issuance contracting 10.2% q-o-q. Indonesia was the sole market in the region that posted declines in issuance on both a q-o-q and a y-o-y basis across all bond segments. The government scaled back its issuance due to higher revenue collections that allowed it to reduce state financing requirements. The government recorded a budget deficit equivalent to 2.4% of GDP in 2022 versus a revised target of 4.5%. In Q4 2022, Bank Indonesia also reduced its issuance of Sukuk Bank Indonesia as the central bank opted to contain inflation by raising policy rates each month from August to December. Corporate bond issuance declined the most among all bond types, as higher borrowing costs curtailed issuance during the quarter.

Table 2: Local Currency Bond Issuance in Select Emerging East Asian Markets (gross)

	Q4 2021		Q3 2022		Q4 2022		Growth Rate (LCY-base %)		Growth Rate (USD-base %)	
	Amount (USD billion)	% share	Amount (USD billion)	% share	Amount (USD billion)	% share	Q4 2022		Q4 2022	
							q-o-q	y-o-y	q-o-q	y-o-y
China, People's Rep. of										
Total	1,598	100.0	1,443	100.0	1,390	100.0	(6.7)	(5.6)	(3.7)	(13.1)
Government	775	48.5	804	55.7	773	55.6	(6.8)	8.2	(3.9)	(0.3)
Central Bank	0	0.0	0	0.0	0	0.0	–	–	–	–
Treasury and Other Govt.	775	48.5	804	55.7	773	55.6	(6.8)	8.2	(3.9)	(0.3)
Corporate	823	51.5	639	44.3	616	44.4	(6.5)	(18.7)	(3.5)	(25.1)
Hong Kong, China										
Total	144	100.0	160	100.0	150	100.0	(6.7)	4.2	(6.1)	4.1
Government	118	81.7	129	80.7	125	83.4	(3.5)	6.3	(2.9)	6.2
Central Bank	117	81.1	123	76.8	124	82.9	0.7	6.5	1.4	6.4
Treasury and Other Govt.	1	0.7	6	3.9	0.8	0.5	(87.8)	(20.0)	(87.7)	(20.1)
Corporate	26	18.3	31	19.3	25	16.6	(19.7)	(5.3)	(19.2)	(5.4)
Indonesia										
Total	49	100.0	44	100.0	39	100.0	(10.2)	(13.0)	(12.2)	(20.4)
Government	47	95.5	41	91.7	37	95.5	(6.5)	(13.0)	(8.5)	(20.3)
Central Bank	28	57.4	23	52.0	22	55.8	(3.6)	(15.4)	(5.7)	(22.5)
Treasury and Other Govt.	19	38.1	18	39.8	15	39.7	(10.3)	(9.4)	(12.2)	(17.0)
Corporate	2	4.5	4	8.3	2	4.5	(51.7)	(13.6)	(52.7)	(20.9)
Korea, Rep. of										
Total	205	100.0	165	100.0	187	100.0	0.3	(3.0)	13.4	(8.9)
Government	60	29.4	61	36.9	55	29.3	(20.5)	(3.6)	(10.1)	(9.4)
Central Bank	21	10.3	19	11.2	19	10.3	(8.2)	(3.4)	3.8	(9.2)
Treasury and Other Govt.	39	19.1	42	25.7	35	19.0	(25.9)	(3.7)	(16.2)	(9.6)
Corporate	145	70.6	104	63.1	132	70.7	12.4	(2.7)	27.1	(8.6)
Malaysia										
Total	21	100.0	26	100.0	27	100.0	0.9	34.1	6.3	26.8
Government	11	53.7	16	63.5	10	38.7	(38.5)	(3.5)	(35.3)	(8.7)
Central Bank	0	0.0	0.9	3.5	0.3	1.0	(71.1)	–	(69.6)	–
Treasury and Other Govt.	11	53.7	15	60.0	10	37.7	(36.6)	(6.0)	(33.3)	(11.1)
Corporate	10	46.3	9	36.5	17	61.3	69.7	77.7	78.7	68.1
Philippines										
Total	39	100.0	49.0	100.0	39	100.0	(24.8)	8.1	(20.8)	(1.1)
Government	38	97.1	47	95.6	36	94.1	(26.0)	4.7	(22.1)	(4.2)
Central Bank	24	60.0	28	58.2	29	75.0	(3.0)	35.0	2.0	23.5
Treasury and Other Govt.	15	37.0	18	37.5	7	19.1	(61.6)	(44.2)	(59.6)	(49.0)
Corporate	1	2.9	2	4.4	2	5.9	1.6	118.1	6.9	99.6
Singapore										
Total	244	100.0	269	100.0	279	100.0	(3.0)	13.8	3.9	14.6
Government	240	98.2	266	99.0	277	99.3	(2.7)	15.0	4.3	15.8
Central Bank	211	86.3	237	88.3	250	89.4	(1.7)	17.8	5.3	18.6
Treasury and Other Govt.	29	11.9	29	10.7	28	9.9	(10.6)	(5.4)	(4.2)	(4.7)
Corporate	4	1.8	3	1.0	2	0.7	(31.9)	(55.0)	(27.0)	(54.6)
Thailand										
Total	61	100.0	59	100.0	64	100.0	(0.3)	7.8	8.7	4.1
Government	50	82.1	44	74.8	49	77.5	3.2	1.8	12.5	(1.7)
Central Bank	31	50.9	28	48.0	31	49.4	2.6	4.7	11.9	1.1
Treasury and Other Govt.	19	31.2	16	26.9	18	28.1	4.2	(2.9)	13.6	(6.3)
Corporate	11	17.9	15	25.2	14	22.5	(10.9)	35.3	(2.8)	30.6

continued on next page

Table 2 *continued*

	Q4 2021		Q3 2022		Q4 2022		Growth Rate (LCY-base %)		Growth Rate (USD-base %)	
	Amount (USD billion)	% share	Amount (USD billion)	% share	Amount (USD billion)	% share	Q4 2022		Q4 2022	
							q-o-q	y-o-y	q-o-q	y-o-y
Viet Nam										
Total	10	100.0	29	100.0	9	100.0	(70.9)	(10.2)	(70.7)	(13.3)
Government	4	42.4	27	92.9	8	98.1	(69.3)	118.9	(69.0)	111.4
Central Bank	0	0.0	25	86.3	4	46.5	(84.3)	–	(84.2)	–
Treasury and Other Govt.	4	42.4	2	6.6	4	51.6	126.8	15.1	129.0	11.2
Corporate	6	57.6	2	7.1	0.2	1.9	(92.3)	(97.2)	(92.2)	(97.3)
Emerging East Asia										
Total	2,371	100.0	2,243	100.0	2,183	100.0	(6.7)	(1.9)	(2.7)	(8.0)
Government	1,343	56.7	1,435	64.0	1,372	62.9	(8.2)	8.0	(4.4)	2.1
Central Bank	431	18.2	484	21.6	480	22.0	(5.6)	12.7	(0.9)	11.3
Treasury and Other Govt.	912	38.5	951	42.4	892	40.9	(9.5)	5.6	(6.1)	(2.2)
Corporate	1,028	43.3	808	36.0	810	37.1	(4.0)	(15.0)	0.3	(21.2)
Japan										
Total	662	100.0	373	100.0	481	100.0	16.7	(17.1)	28.9	(27.3)
Government	615	93.0	347	92.9	448	93.1	17.0	(17.0)	29.1	(27.1)
Central Bank	0	0.0	0	0.0	0	0.0	–	–	–	–
Treasury and Other Govt.	615	93.0	347	92.9	448	93.1	17.0	(17.0)	29.1	(27.1)
Corporate	47	7.0	26	7.1	33	6.9	13.4	(19.2)	25.2	(29.1)

( ) = negative, – = not applicable, LCY = local currency, q-o-q = quarter-on-quarter, Q2 = second quarter, Q3 = third quarter, USD = United States dollar, y-o-y = year-on-year.

Notes:
1. Corporate bonds include issues by financial institutions.
2. Bloomberg LP end-of-period LCY–USD rates are used.
3. For LCY base, emerging East Asia growth figures are based on 31 December 2022 currency exchange rates and do not include currency effects.

Sources: People's Republic of China (CEIC Data Company); Hong Kong, China (Hong Kong Monetary Authority); Indonesia (Bank Indonesia; Directorate General of Budget Financing and Risk Management, Ministry of Finance; and Indonesia Stock Exchange); Republic of Korea (KG Zeroin Corporation and The Bank of Korea); Malaysia (Bank Negara Malaysia); Philippines (Bureau of the Treasury and Bloomberg LP); Singapore (Monetary Authority of Singapore and Bloomberg LP); Thailand (Bank of Thailand); Viet Nam (Bloomberg LP, Hanoi Stock Exchange, and Vietnam Bond Market Association); and Japan (Japan Securities Dealers Association).

In the Philippines, bond issuance plunged 24.8% q-o-q in Q4 2022, with aggregate issuance reaching USD38.8 billion. The slowdown in issuance was largely driven by a substantial decline in government bonds due to a high-base effect from the previous quarter when the government's issuance of Retail Treasury Bonds soared. Issuance by the BSP also contracted as it continued to raise policy rates to rein in inflation. The BSP was the most aggressive central bank in the region in terms of raising policy rates in 2022. Meanwhile, the corporate bond segment posted marginal issuance growth of 1.6% q-o-q in Q4 2022.

LCY bond issuance in Malaysia recorded marginal growth of 0.9% q-o-q in Q4 2022 to reach USD27.1 billion, buoyed by increased issuance in the corporate bond segment. Corporate bond sales nearly doubled, climbing 69.7% q-o-q in Q4 2022 after a decline of 0.7% q-o-q in the prior quarter. On the other hand, government bond issuance substantially declined over reduced issuance by the central government and the central bank.

In Viet Nam, LCY bond issuance declined the most among ASEAN peers in Q4 2022 with a contraction of 70.9% q-o-q, but this was largely due to a high base effect. Total issuance declined to USD8.6 billion amid a deceleration in issuance by both the central bank and corporate segments. Corporate bond issuance slumped as liquidity constraints dragged issuance, making it difficult for issuers to raise funds from the bond market or refinance maturing obligations. Meanwhile, issuance of Treasury and other government bonds more than doubled in Q4 2022.

Cross-Border Bond Issuance

Cross-border bond issuance in emerging East Asia reached USD12.0 billion in Q4 2022.

Emerging East Asia's cross-border bond issuance in Q4 2022 reached USD12.0 billion, reflecting a 46.0% q-o-q increase from the USD8.2 billion raised in the previous quarter. The higher issuance volume was largely driven by the Republic of Korea, whose bond issuance increased more than tenfold in Q4 2022. Other economies that registered cross-border bond issuances in the same quarter were Malaysia and Hong Kong, China, which both recorded a decline in the issuance of intra-regional bonds in Q4 2022, as well as Cambodia, which issued its sole cross-border bond for 2022. Monthly issuance volumes amounted to USD1.9 billion, USD9.5 billion, and USD0.7 billion in October, November, and December, respectively. Compared with Q4 2021, total cross-border bond issuance increased almost threefold from USD4.1 billion.

The Republic of Korea's cross-border bond issuance volume increased significantly in Q4 2022, garnering a regional market share of 68.1% and topping Hong Kong, China, which had the largest market share in the previous quarter (**Figure 9**). The Republic of Korea's cross-border issuance in Q4 2022 totaled USD8.2 billion, posing a notable jump of 932.3% q-o-q from USD0.8 billion in Q3 2022. During the quarter, eight institutions from the Republic of Korea issued cross-border bonds that were denominated in three different currencies: Chinese yuan, Hong Kong dollars, and Singapore dollars. KB Capital, a publicly listed company that engages in personal and corporate financial services in the Republic of Korea raised a total of USD7.2 billion via issuance of a 2-year CNY-denominated bond, making it the largest issuer of cross-border bonds and the single-largest issuance in both the Republic of Korea and the region in Q4 2022. Korea Hydro & Nuclear Power Company was the second largest cross-border

bond issuer during the quarter, raising USD0.3 billion via issuance of a 10-year HKD-denominated bond. Another notable issuer was Korea Expressway with a total issuance volume of USD0.2 billion comprising three tranches denominated in Hong Kong dollars and Singapore dollars. The Export–Import Bank of Korea raised USD0.1 billion via issuance of multitranche HKD-denominated bonds in Q4 2022.

Hong Kong, China was the second-largest issuer of cross-border bonds in emerging East Asia during Q4 2022, with an aggregate issuance volume of USD3.8 billion for a 31.2% share of the regional cross-border bond issuance total during the quarter. This represented a significant decline of 43.5% q-o-q from USD6.6 billion of intra-regional bond issuance in Q3 2022. During the review period, 14 firms issued intra-regional bonds in Hong Kong, China, which were all denominated in Chinese yuan. Transportation and financial companies were the top issuers of intra-regional bonds in Hong Kong, China during Q4 2022, with shares of 53.0% and 38.5%, respectively. China Merchants Group, a state-owned enterprise engaged in logistics services, raised USD1.9 billion via issuance of a triple-tranche bond, making it the largest issuer of cross-border bonds in Hong Kong, China and the second-largest issuer in emerging East Asia in Q4 2022. Other notable issuers came from financial companies, including Hong Kong Mortgage Corporation and Bocom Leasing Management Hong Kong Company, which raised USD0.5 billion via issuance of a multitranche bond and USD0.3 billion via issuance of a 3-year bond, respectively.

In Malaysia, Cagamas Global was the sole issuer of intra-regional bonds in Q4 2022, raising USD48.5 million worth of 1-year bonds denominated in Singapore dollars. In the same quarter, Hattha Bank was the only issuer of cross-border bonds from Cambodia, successfully raising USD43.3 million via issuance of a 3-year bond denominated in Thai baht.

The top 10 issuers of intra-regional bonds in Q4 2022 had an aggregate issuance volume of USD11.2 billion and accounted for 93.2% of the regional total. Four of the firms were from the Republic of Korea, with aggregate issuance of USD7.9 billion, and the remaining six firms were from Hong Kong, China, with a total volume of USD3.3 billion. The top issuer was financial firm KB Capital based in the Republic of Korea, followed by two firms from Hong Kong, China: China Merchants

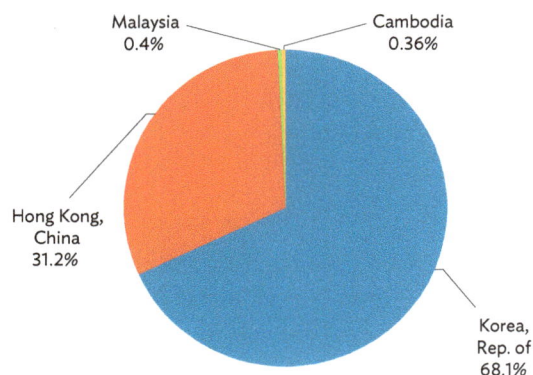

Figure 9: Origin Economies of Select Intra-Emerging East Asian Bond Issuance in the Fourth Quarter of 2022

Malaysia 0.4%
Cambodia 0.36%
Hong Kong, China 31.2%
Korea, Rep. of 68.1%

Source: *AsianBondsOnline* calculations based on Bloomberg LP data.

Group and Hong Kong Mortgage Corporation, which are engaged in the transportation and finance industries, respectively. Financial firms comprised six of the top 10 cross-border bond issuers in Q4 2022.

The Chinese yuan continued to be the most widely used currency for cross-border bond issuance in Q4 2022, with an aggregate issuance volume of USD11,135.2 million or 92.5% of the regional total (**Figure 10**). Institutions from the Republic of Korea and Hong Kong, China issued intra-regional bonds denominated in Chinese yuan. Other issuances were carried out in Hong Kong dollars (USD649.6 million), Singapore dollars (USD214.3 million), and Thai baht (USD43.3 million), which accounted for regional shares of 5.4%, 1.8%, and 0.4%, respectively. Cambodia was the only market that issued cross-border bonds denominated in Thai baht.

Figure 10: Currency Shares of Select Intra-Emerging East Asian Bond Issuance in the Fourth Quarter of 2022

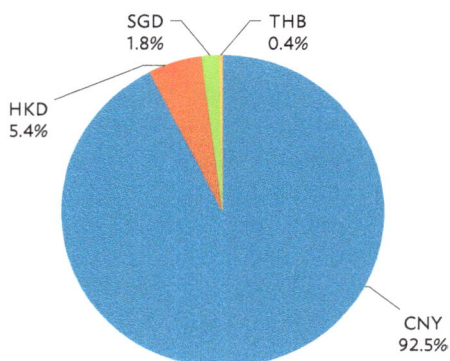

CNY = Chinese yuan, HKD = Hong Kong dollar, SGD = Singapore dollar, THB = Thai baht.
Source: *AsianBondsOnline* calculations based on Bloomberg LP data.

In Q4 2022, issuance of intra-regional bonds in emerging East Asia was largely dominated by the financial sector with an aggregate issuance volume of USD9.1 billion, comprising 75.3% of the regional total (**Figure 11**). The financial sector was the only sector that posted a quarterly increase in its regional issuance share, exhibiting a significant jump of 257.5% q-o-q from USD2.5 billion in Q3 2022. The transportation sector was the second-largest issuer group of cross-border bonds in the same quarter, with total issuance of USD2.2 billion and a

Figure 11: Select Intra-Emerging East Asian Bond Issuance by Sector

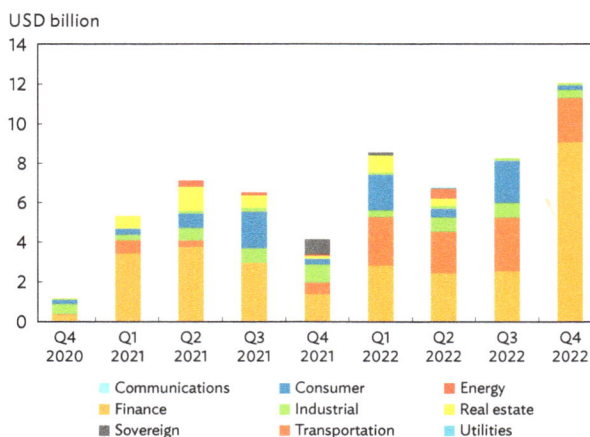

Q1 = first quarter, Q2 = second quarter, Q3 = third quarter, Q4 = fourth quarter, USD = United States dollar.
Note: Figures were computed based on 31 December 2022 exchange rates to avoid currency effects.
Source: *AsianBondsOnline* calculations based on Bloomberg LP data.

regional share of 18.5%. The third-largest group was the utilities sector at USD0.4 billion and a share of 3.4% of the regional total.

G3 Currency Issuance

Emerging East Asian markets raised G3 currency bonds totaling USD222.1 billion in 2022.

G3 currency bonds worth USD222.1 billion were issued by emerging East Asia in 2022 (**Figure 12**).[8] This represented a decline of 41.0% y-o-y from the USD376.4 billion raised in 2021. All economies in the region registered a decline in total G3 currency bonds issued during the review period. These contractions were due to aggressive rate hikes throughout the year by the United States (US) Federal Reserve giving rise to a strong US dollar. The higher borrowing costs led to fewer entities in all economies in the region issuing G3 currency bonds in 2022.

In 2022, 92.2% of the total value of emerging East Asia's issuance of G3 currency bonds was denominated in US dollars, 6.5% in euros, and 1.3% in Japanese yen. USD-denominated bonds issued during 2022 totaled

---

[8] G3 currency bonds are denominated in either euros, Japanese yen, or United States dollars.

Figure 12: G3 Currency Bond Issuance in Select Emerging East Asian Markets

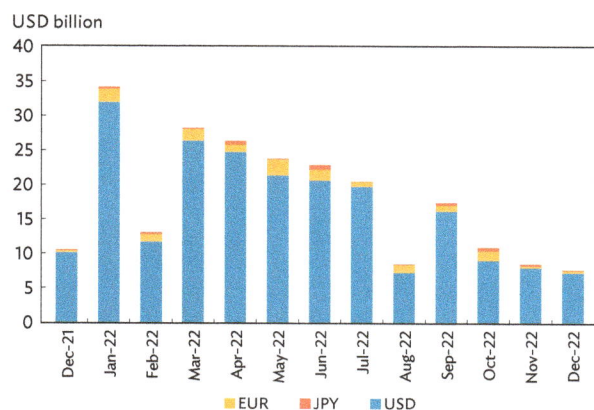

USD billion

EUR = euro, JPY = Japanese yen, USD = United States dollar.

Notes:
1. G3 currency bonds are denominated in either euros, Japanese yen, or United States dollars.
2. Figures were computed based on 31 December 2022 currency exchange rates and do not include currency effects.

Source: *AsianBondsOnline* calculations based on Bloomberg LP data.

USD204.7 billion, falling 40.5% y-o-y from 2021 due to reduced fundraising activities from all markets in the region. Issuances denominated in euros totaled USD14.5 billion on a contraction of 52.1% y-o-y due to a y-o-y drop in issuances from the PRC and the Republic of Korea, as well as the absence of any fundraising in euros from Hong Kong, China; Indonesia; and the Philippines. G3 currency bonds denominated in Japanese yen amounted to USD3.0 billion, an expansion of 36.0% y-o-y as the Republic of Korea, Malaysia, and the Philippines issued more samurai bonds, and the PRC resumed issuances in Japanese yen in 2022.

In terms of G3 currency bond issuance in 2022, entities from the PRC led emerging East Asia with total issuance equivalent to USD127.6 billion (**Table 3**). A distant second was the Republic of Korea with USD41.7 billion. Hong Kong, China followed with USD15.3 billion. All economies in the region continued to issue most of their G3 currency bonds in US dollars in 2022.

In 2022, 57.4% of total sales in G3 currency bonds in the region came from entities in the PRC: USD119.4 billion in US dollars, USD8.0 billion worth of issuances in euros, and the equivalent of USD0.2 billion in Japanese yen. In November and December, Huatai International Financial Holdings issued nine USD-denominated bonds

totaling USD0.3 billion with tenors ranging from 3 months to 4 years.

The Republic of Korea had a share of 18.8% of the overall G3 currency bond issuance in emerging East Asia in 2022: US dollar issuance was USD36.8 billion; the equivalent of USD3.8 billion was EUR-denominated; and a total of USD1.1 billion was issued in Japanese yen, an 828.0% increase in JPY-denominated issuance from 2021. At the beginning of October, Korea Electric Power Corporation issued dual-tranche, USD-denominated green bonds totaling USD0.8 billion. The green bonds had tenors of 3.5 years and 5.5 years, proceeds of which will be used for financing green projects under the company's sustainable finance framework. Before October ended, Hyundai Capital Services had raised a total of USD0.2 billion from a triple-tranche issuance of samurai bonds with tenors of 1.5 years, 2 years, and 3 years. The privately placed bond was the first samurai bond issuance by the company since 2018.

Hong Kong, China accounted for 6.9% of G3 currency bond issuance in the region in 2022. This comprised USD-denominated bonds amounting to USD15.2 billion and the equivalent of USD0.1 billion in Japanese yen. There were no EUR-denominated issuances in Hong Kong, China in 2022. In October, insurance company AIA Group issued a USD-denominated callable bond with a tenor of 5 years amounting to USD0.9 billion. In November, the Hong Kong Mortgage Corporation raised funds through a 1-year USD-denominated bond worth USD0.1 billion.

Issuance of bonds in G3 currencies in the ASEAN region declined 50.2% y-o-y in 2022 as such issuance from all economies contracted during the year. A combined USD37.5 billion of G3 currency bonds were issued by entities based in the region in 2022. This was less than the USD75.4 billion registered in 2021. Markets from the ASEAN region had a share of 16.9% of emerging East Asia's G3 currency bond issuance in 2022, a decline from 20.0% in the previous year. During the review period, the economy with the most G3 currency bond issuance in the ASEAN region was Indonesia, trailed by Singapore, Malaysia, the Philippines, and Thailand.

Issuance of G3 currency bonds in Indonesia in 2022 accounted for 5.5% of the total in emerging East Asia. A majority of Indonesia's G3 currency bond issuances

Table 3: G3 Currency Bond Issuance in Select Asian Markets

2021			2022		
Issuer	**Amount (USD billion)**	**Issue Date**	**Issuer**	**Amount (USD billion)**	**Issue Date**
China, People's Rep. of	**217.4**		**China, People's Rep. of**	**127.6**	
Industrial and Commercial Bank of China 3.200% Perpetual	6.2	24-Sep-21	Easy Tactic 7.50% 2027	2.3	11-Jul-22
China Development Bank 0.380% 2022	2.0	10-Jun-21	China Construction Bank 2.85% 2032	2.0	21-Jan-22
Prosus 3.061% 2031	1.9	13-Jul-21	Easy Tactic 7.50% 2028	1.7	11-Jul-22
Others	207.4		Others	121.7	
Hong Kong, China	**39.7**		**Hong Kong, China**	**15.3**	
Hong Kong, China (Sovereign) 0.000% 2026	1.4	24-Nov-21	Airport Authority Hong Kong 2.50% 2032	1.2	12-Jan-22
NWD Finance 4.125% Perpetual	1.2	10-Jun-21	Airport Authority Hong Kong 3.25% 2052	1.2	12-Jan-22
Hong Kong, China (Sovereign) 0.625% 2026	1.0	2-Feb-21	Airport Authority Hong Kong 1.75% 2027	1.0	12-Jan-22
Others	36.1		Others	11.9	
Indonesia	**26.4**		**Indonesia**	**12.2**	
Indonesia (Sovereign) 3.05% 2051	2.0	12-Jan-21	Perusahaan Penerbit SBSN Indonesia III 4.400% 2027	1.8	6-Jun-22
Perusahaan Penerbit SBSN Indonesia III 1.50% 2026	1.3	9-Jun-21	Freeport Indonesia 5.315% 2032	1.5	14-Apr-22
Indonesia (Sovereign) 1.85% 2031	1.3	12-Jan-21	Perusahaan Penerbit SBSN Indonesia III 4.700% 2032	1.5	6-Jun-22
Others	21.9		Others	7.4	
Korea, Rep. of	**43.9**		**Korea, Rep. of**	**41.7**	
Posco 0.00% 2026	1.2	1-Sep-21	Export-Import Bank of Korea 1.375% 2025	1.1	24-May-22
Korea Housing Finance Corporation 0.01% 2026	1.1	29-Jun-21	Korea Development Bank 2.000% 2025	1.0	24-Feb-22
SK Hynix 1.50% 2026	1.0	19-Jan-21	Export-Import Bank of Korea 4.250% 2027	1.0	15-Sep-22
Others	40.6		Others	38.6	
Malaysia	**16.0**		**Malaysia**	**7.5**	
Petronas Capital 3.404% 2061	1.8	28-Apr-21	MISC Capital Two (Labuan) 3.75% 2027	0.6	6-Apr-22
Petronas Capital 2.480% 2032	1.3	28-Apr-21	Bank Negara Interbank Bills 0.00% 2022	0.6	25-Jan-22
Others	13.0		Others	6.3	
Philippines	**10.8**		**Philippines**	**4.8**	
Philippines (Sovereign) 3.200% 2046	2.3	6-Jul-21	Philippines (Sovereign) 4.20% 2047	1.0	29-Mar-22
Philippines (Sovereign) 1.375% 2026	1.1	8-Oct-21	Philippines (Sovereign) 5.95% 2047	0.8	13-Oct-22
Others	7.5		Others	3.0	
Singapore	**16.5**		**Singapore**	**10.7**	
BOC Aviation 1.625% 2024	1.0	29-Apr-21	United Overseas Bank 0.387% 2025	1.6	17-Mar-22
Temasek Financial I 2.750% 2061	1.0	2-Aug-21	DBS Bank 2.375% 2027	1.5	17-Mar-22
Others	14.5		Others	7.6	
Thailand	**4.1**		**Thailand**	**2.4**	
Bangkok Bank in Hong Kong, China 3.466% 2036	1.0	23-Sep-21	GC Treasury Center 4.4% 2032	1.0	30-Mar-22
GC Treasury Center 2.980% 2031	0.7	18-Mar-21	Bangkok Bank in Hong Kong, China 4.3% 2027	0.8	15-Jun-22
Others	2.4		Others	0.7	
Viet Nam	**1.6**		**Viet Nam**	**–**	
Emerging East Asia Total	**376.4**		**Emerging East Asia Total**	**222.1**	
Memo Items:			**Memo Items:**		
India	**23.7**		**India**	**8.3**	
Vedanta Resources 8.95% 2025	1.2	11-Mar-21	Reliance Industries 3.625% 2052	1.8	12-Jan-22
Others	22.5		Others	6.5	
Sri Lanka	**0.8**		**Sri Lanka**	**0.01**	
Sri Lanka (Sovereign) 7.95% 2024	0.2	3-May-21	Sri Lanka (Sovereign) 8% 2023	0.01	24-Jan-22
Others	0.6		Others	0.002	

USD = United States dollar.

Notes:
1. Data exclude certificates of deposit.
2. G3 currency bonds are bonds denominated in either euros, Japanese yen, or United States dollars.
3. Bloomberg LP end-of-period rates are used.
4. Figures after the issuer name reflect the coupon rate and year of maturity of the bond.

Source: *AsianBondsOnline* calculations based on Bloomberg LP data.

were in US dollars, amounting to USD11.5 billion, while the equivalent of USD0.6 billion were in Japanese yen. No EUR-denominated bonds were issued by Indonesia in 2022. In December, township developer Kawasan Industri Jababeka issued a 5-year callable bond denominated in US dollars worth USD0.2 billion. Proceeds from the issuance will be used to pay off part of the company's existing senior notes worth USD0.3 billion. Just before 2022 ended, Indonesia's flag air carrier Garuda Indonesia issued a USD-denominated callable Islamic bond worth USD0.08 billion with tenor of 9 years, as part of its debt restructuring plan. The company defaulted in 2021 on its *sukuk* following difficulties caused by the COVID-19 pandemic and related air travel restrictions.

Singapore had a 4.8% share of the region's G3 currency bond issuance during the review period. Entities from Singapore raised USD7.9 billion denominated in US dollars, the equivalent of USD2.6 billion in euros, and JPY-denominated securities worth USD0.2 billion. Unlike issuances in Japanese yen and the US dollar, EUR-denominated bond issuances increased in 2022 compared to the prior year. In October, DBS Bank issued a 3-year EUR-denominated covered bond worth USD0.8 billion. Toward the end of November, most investors in coal mining company Golden Energy and Resources' existing bonds due in 2026 swapped the bonds for a 5-year callable USD-denominated bond worth USD0.3 billion. The swap allowed the company to restructure its coal energy business.

Issuers in Malaysia raised 3.4% of the total G3 currency bonds issued in emerging East Asia in 2022. Issuances in USD-denominated bonds totaled USD7.3 billion, while JPY-denominated bonds reached the equivalent of USD0.2 billion, more than double from the previous year. These bonds denominated in Japanese yen were issued by Malayan Banking in February. During Q4 2022, Bank Negara Malaysia issued five Bank Negara Interbank Bills. These zero-coupon short-term securities are used by the central bank for liquidity management purposes.

Issuers from the Philippines comprised a 2.2% share of total issuance of regional G3 currency bonds in 2022. By currency, entities from the Philippines raised USD4.3 billion worth of bonds denominated in US dollars and the equivalent of USD0.5 billion in Japanese yen. JPY-denominated issuances increased, while USD-denominated bonds decreased in 2022.

The Philippines had no euro issuances during the year. In October, the Government of the Philippines issued three tranches of USD-denominated Global Bonds with tenors of 5 years, 10.5 years, and 25 years. Proceeds from the 5-year and 10.5-year bonds will be utilized for general purposes, while funds raised from the 25-year tenor will be used for the Philippines' projects under its Sustainable Finance Framework.

A 1.1% share of emerging East Asian G3 currency bond issuance in 2022 came from Thailand. These bonds, all of which were denominated in US dollars for a total of USD2.4 billion, were issued in March and June.

Bond Yield Movements

Yields in most emerging East Asian markets declined as the Federal Reserve slowed the pace of its monetary tightening.

While most advanced economy central banks have largely continued their monetary policy tightening as global inflation remains elevated, there are some signs of a gradual shifting or pivot.

In the US, the Federal Reserve, during its 1–2 November meeting, raised its policy rate target range by 75 bps but also announced that it would reduce the pace of its rate hikes. Following this, the Federal Reserve raised its policy rate target range by only 50 bps on 14–15 December and by an even smaller 25 bps each, at its 31 January–1 February and 21–22 March meetings.

Similar to the Federal Reserve, the European Central Bank softened the pace of its rate hikes. In the euro area, the European Central Bank raised its policy rates by 75 bps on 27 October. It followed this up with successive and smaller 50 bps rate hike on 15 December, 2 February, and 16 March.

The Bank of Japan has largely kept monetary policy accommodative, but during its 20 December meeting it adjusted the band by which it allows the 10-year Japanese Government Bond to fluctuate from ±0.25% to ±0.50%. This led to market speculation that the Bank of Japan would soon be exiting from its accommodative policy. However, expectations were dashed when on 10 March, the Bank of Japan left monetary policy unchanged, keeping policy rates and the Japanese Government Bonds trading band steady.

While a Federal Reserve shift has improved market optimism and led yields to largely decline in emerging East Asia, volatility increased from 1 February through 10 March. The Federal Reserve minutes of the January meeting, coupled with strong January nonfarm payroll data, heightened concerns that the Federal Reserve may raise policy rates in March by 50 bps as opposed to the previously expected 25 bps. However, the closure of Silicon Valley Bank on 10 March drove contagion fears and, while it has largely negatively impacted equity markets in the region, changed market expectations of a softer Federal Reserve move.

As a result, while 2-year yields largely trended downward starting at the end of November 2022, yields began rising again from 1 February through 10 March, except for the PRC (**Figure 13a**). In the PRC, rising yields were driven by speculation in November that the PRC would be reopening its economy. Subsequently, the PRC announced on 7 December that it would be moving away from its zero COVID policy. On 26 December, the PRC announced that it would ease quarantine measures for foreign travelers effective 8 January 2023. In contrast, other markets had more dramatic declines in yields from November onward, before exhibiting the same upward movement from 1 February through 10 March. Yield movements in Malaysia and Thailand, however, were more muted from 30 November to 10 March in comparison to its peers (**Figure 13b**).

Yields on the region's 10-year bonds largely exhibited similar trends, declining in November before rising again from 1 February to 10 March, with the PRC being the exception as its 10-year yield was largely stable (**Figure 14a**). Meanwhile, Thailand's 10-year yield did not exhibit as strong as a rise in 1 February-10 March period compared to its peers (**Figure 14b**).

Yield curves in most markets in emerging East Asia shifted downward between 30 November and 10 March (**Figure 15**). Only Singapore's and the PRC's yield curves rose for most tenors. In the PRC, yields rose following the end of the PRC's zero COVID policy. The continued tightening of central banks in the region has begun to take effect, with speculation that, globally, most central banks are near the end of their tightening cycle. The GDP of regional economies has been impacted by the tightening phase, and Q4 2022 GDP growth rates slowed for all markets in the region. The largest GDP slowdowns were seen in the Republic of Korea, Malaysia, Thailand, and Viet Nam, which posted growth rates less than half of their previous quarter growth rates. In contrast to the rest of the region, Hong Kong, China's GDP continued to contract in Q4 2022, affected by zero COVID measures in the PRC as well as a weak external environment.

Inflation also began to decline in most markets during Q4 2022 amid continued monetary tightening as well as declining commodity prices globally. The exceptions to

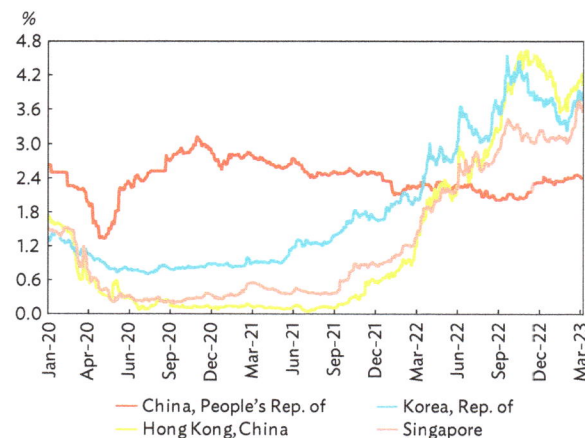

Figure 13a: 2-Year Local Currency Government Bond Yields

%

Note: Data coverage is from 1 January 2020 to 10 March 2023.
Source: Based on data from Bloomberg LP.

Legend: China, People's Rep. of; Hong Kong, China; Korea, Rep. of; Singapore

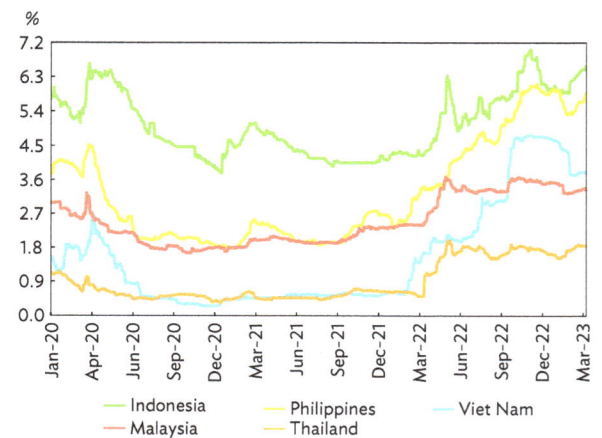

Figure 13b: 2-Year Local Currency Government Bond Yields

%

Note: Data coverage is from 1 January 2020 to 10 March 2023.
Source: Based on data from Bloomberg LP.

Legend: Indonesia; Malaysia; Philippines; Thailand; Viet Nam

Figure 14a: 10-Year Local Currency Government Bond Yields

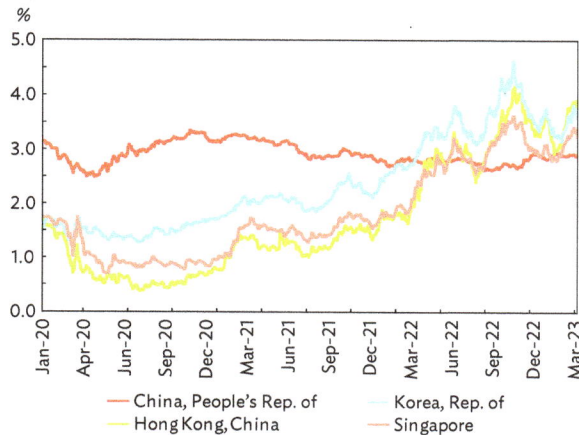

Note: Data coverage is from 1 January 2020 to 10 March 2023.
Source: Based on data from Bloomberg LP.

Figure 14b: 10-Year Local Currency Government Bond Yields

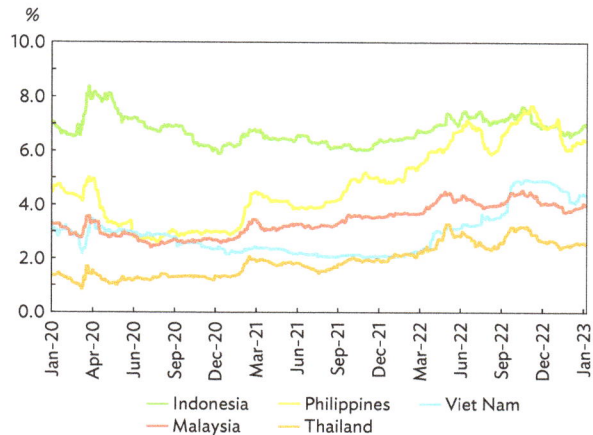

Note: Data coverage is from 1 January 2020 to 10 March 2023.
Source: Based on data from Bloomberg LP.

the declining trend in inflation were Hong Kong, China, where inflation accelerated following the opening of its economy, and also Viet Nam, as its central bank was slower to tighten monetary policy than its regional peers (**Figure 16a**). The Philippines was also an exception as the economy continued to grapple with higher food prices (**Figure 16b**).

As a result, the BSP remained vigilant in tightening monetary policy. During the November–January period, the BSP was the most aggressive, having raised rates by a total of 125 bps. It followed up on this with another 50 bps rate hike on 16 February (**Figure 17a**). Indonesia was the next most aggressive with a cumulative 100 bps rate hike during the review period, but it kept its policy rate steady in its February and March meetings (**Figure 17b**). Interestingly, the State Bank of Vietnam, after having consecutive 100 bps rate hikes in September and October, kept its refinancing rate steady at 6.00% on 14 March, but cut its overnight and rediscounting rates by 100 bps each to support economic recovery.

Corporate spreads rose for lower-rated corporate bonds.

The spread between AAA-rated yields and government yields declined in emerging East Asian markets for which data are available (**Figure 18a**). In contrast, lower-rated credit spreads widened in most markets as rising funding costs highlighted concerns over funding for riskier corporates (**Figure 18b**).

Figure 15: Benchmark Yield Curves—Local Currency Government Bonds

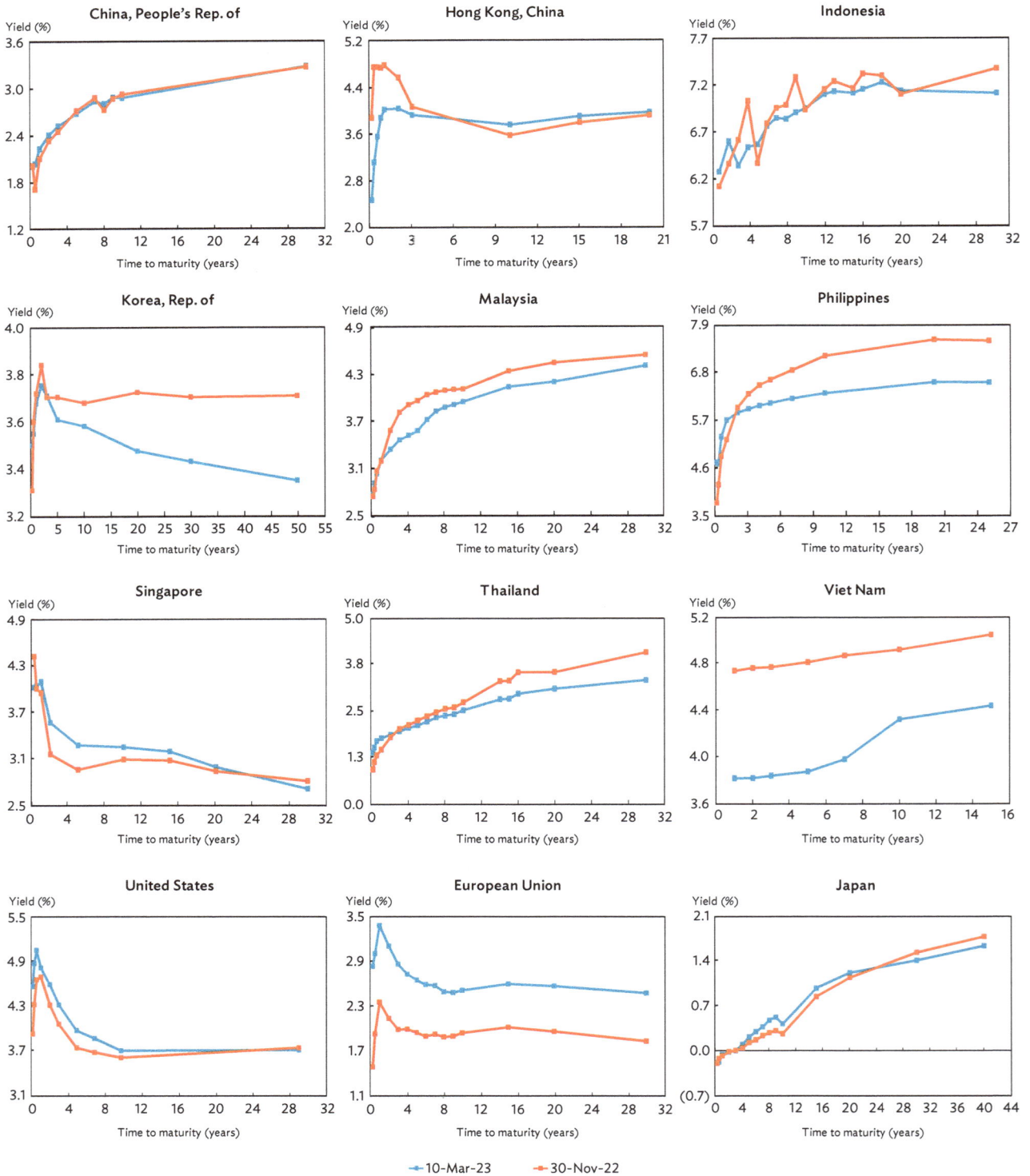

China, People's Rep. of

Yield (%)

Time to maturity (years)

Hong Kong, China

Yield (%)

Time to maturity (years)

Indonesia

Yield (%)

Time to maturity (years)

Korea, Rep. of

Yield (%)

Time to maturity (years)

Malaysia

Yield (%)

Time to maturity (years)

Philippines

Yield (%)

Time to maturity (years)

Singapore

Yield (%)

Time to maturity (years)

Thailand

Yield (%)

Time to maturity (years)

Viet Nam

Yield (%)

Time to maturity (years)

United States

Yield (%)

Time to maturity (years)

European Union

Yield (%)

Time to maturity (years)

Japan

Yield (%)

Time to maturity (years)

— 10-Mar-23   — 30-Nov-22

( ) = negative.
Sources: Based on data from Bloomberg LP and Thai Bond Market Association.

Figure 16a: Headline Inflation Rates

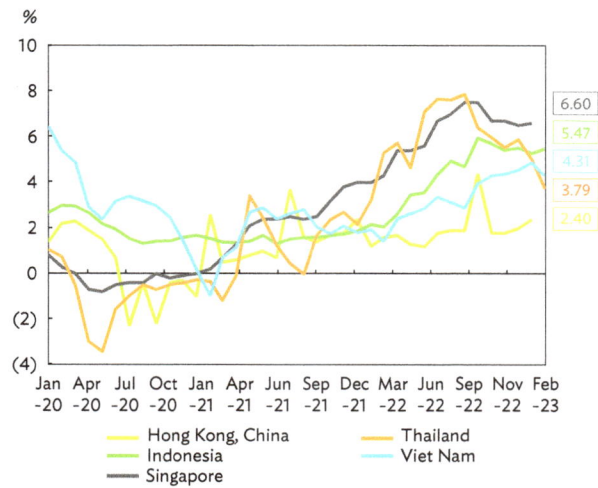

Note: Data coverage is from January 2020 to February 2023 except for Hong Kong, China and Singapore (January 2023).
Source: Based on data from Bloomberg LP.

Figure 16b: Headline Inflation Rates

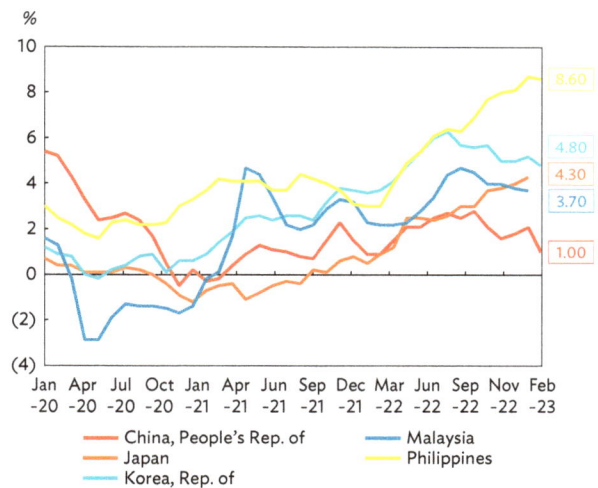

Note: Data coverage is from January 2020 to February 2023 except for Japan and Malaysia (January 2023).
Source: Based on data from Bloomberg LP.

Figure 17a: Policy Rates

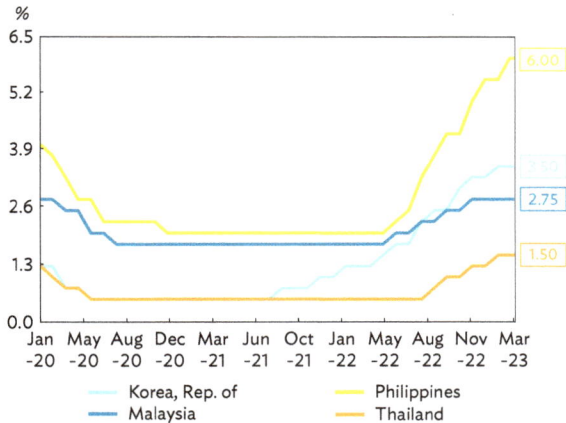

Note: Data coverage is from 31 January 2020 to 10 March 2023.
Source: Based on data from Bloomberg LP.

Figure 17b: Policy Rates

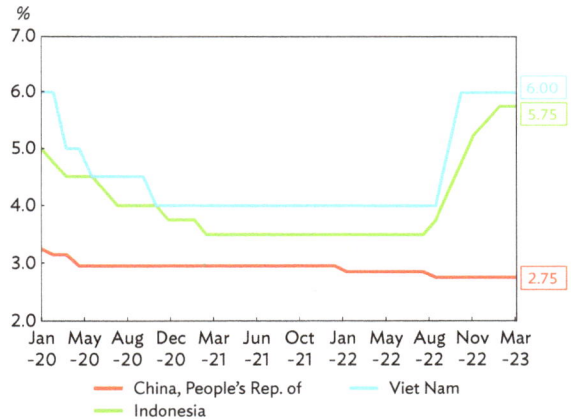

Notes:
1. Data coverage is from 31 January 2020 to 10 March 2023.
2. For the People's Republic of China, data used in the chart are the 1-year medium-term lending facility rate. While the 1-year benchmark lending rate is the official policy rate of the People's Bank of China, market players use the 1-year medium-term lending facility rate as a guide for the monetary policy direction of the People's Bank of China.

Source: Based on data from Bloomberg LP.

Figure 18a: Credit Spreads—Local Currency Corporates Rated AAA versus Government Bonds

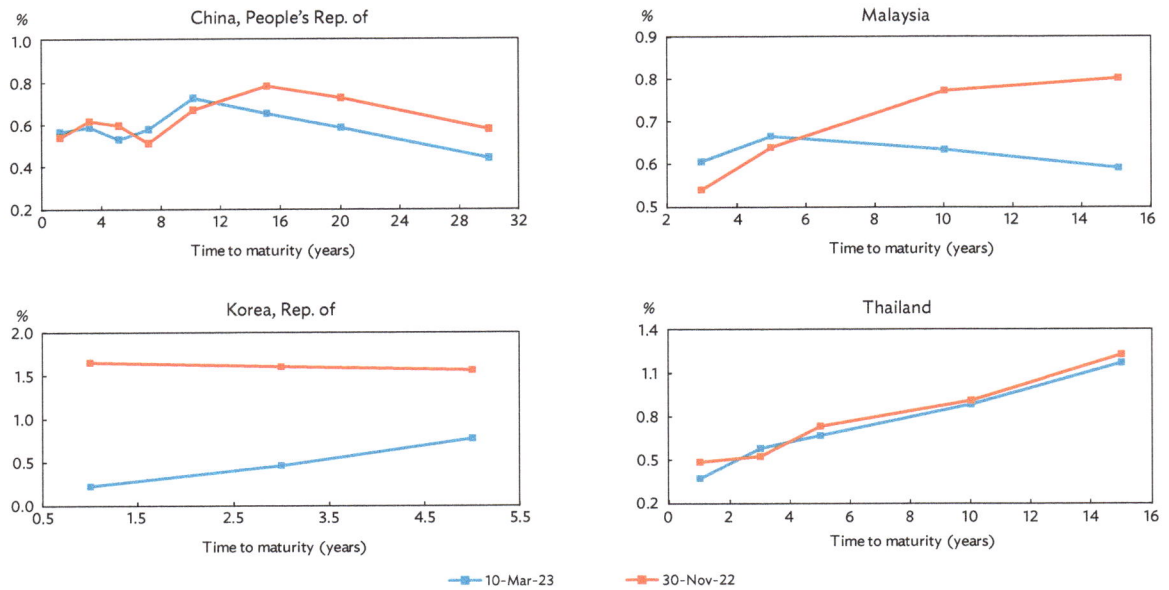

Notes:
1. Credit spreads are obtained by subtracting government yields from corporate indicative yields.
2. Corporate yields for Malaysia are as of 30 November 2022 and 7 March 2023.

Sources: People's Republic of China (Bloomberg LP), Republic of Korea (KG Zeroin Corporation), Malaysia (Fully Automated System for Issuing/Tendering Bank Negara Malaysia), and Thailand (Bloomberg LP).

Figure 18b: Credit Spreads—Lower-Rated Local Currency Corporates versus AAA

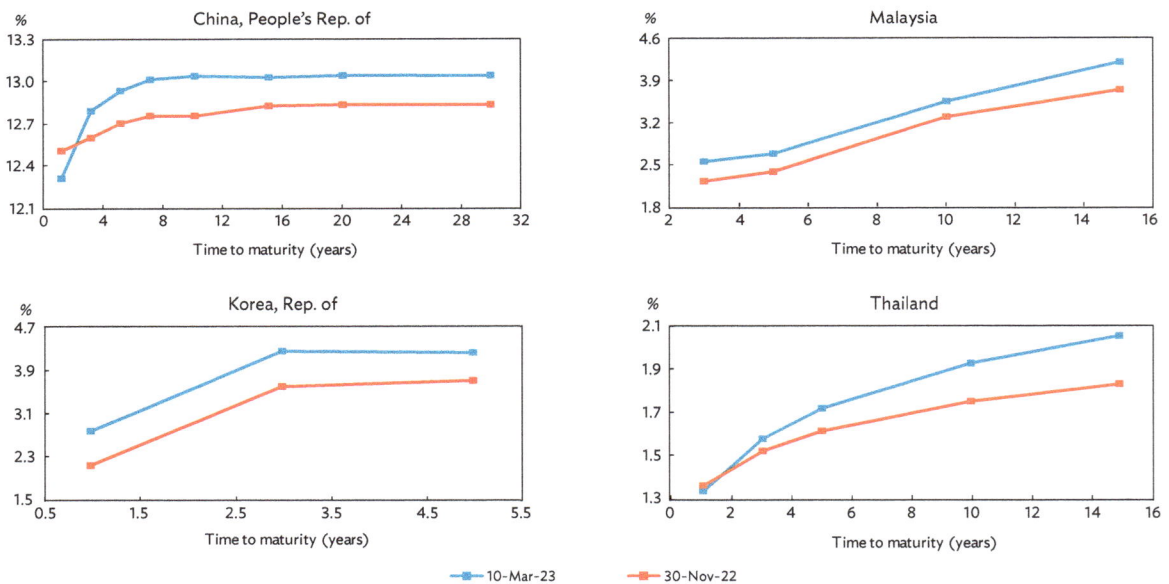

Notes:
1. Credit spreads are obtained by subtracting government yields from corporate indicative yields.
2. Corporate yields for Malaysia are as of 30 November 2022 and 7 March 2023.

Sources: People's Republic of China (Bloomberg LP), Republic of Korea (KG Zeroin Corporation), Malaysia (Fully Automated System for Issuing/Tendering Bank Negara Malaysia), and Thailand (Bloomberg LP).

Recent Developments in ASEAN+3 Sustainable Bond Markets

Sustainable bonds in ASEAN+3 markets expanded at a faster pace than the global average in 2022, but they still accounted for a limited share of the region's overall bond market.[9] The sustainable bond market in ASEAN+3 reached a size of USD589.3 billion at the end of 2022 on year-on-year (y-o-y) growth of 36.7%. While growth was slower compared to the 53.8% y-o-y expansion in 2021, due to tightening financial conditions, ASEAN+3's bond market posted a faster expansion than global sustainable bond markets, which totaled USD3.3 trillion at the end of 2022 on growth of 27.2% y-o-y. Rapid growth has been partially driven by investor interest in the diversification benefits of sustainable bonds. **Box 5** delves into this aspect much more deeply. ASEAN+3 remains the second-largest regional sustainable bond market in the world, representing a 17.7% share of the global aggregate, next to the European Union 20 (EU-20) (**Figure 19**). Nevertheless, ASEAN+3's sustainable bond market accounted for only 1.7% of ASEAN+3's aggregate bonds outstanding at the end of 2022, which was below sustainable bonds' 3.0% share of total global bonds outstanding.

The ASEAN+3 sustainable bond market is dominated by green bonds (65.6%), local currency (LCY) financing (64.7%), and private sector financing (77.8%) (**Figure 20**). ASEAN markets accounted for 8.0% of the wider region's sustainable bond stock, compared with 6.2% of ASEAN+3's overall bond market. With a weighted average remaining tenor of 4.5 years, 54.2% of ASEAN+3 sustainable bonds have a remaining tenor of less than 3 years, compared to an average of 7.5 years in the overall bond market of ASEAN+3.

Growth in sustainable bond issuance moderated in 2022 on monetary tightening globally and in the region. ASEAN+3's sustainable bond issuance totaled USD231.5 billion in 2022, with growth decelerating to 5.9% y-o-y from 147.9% y-o-y in 2021 (**Figure 21**). ASEAN+3's share of global sustainable bond issuance rose to 27.2% in 2022, up from 19.2% in 2021. Sustainable bond issuance in ASEAN markets grew 25.1% y-o-y, the second-fastest growth rate in ASEAN+3 after the People's Republic of China (PRC), driven largely by increased issuance from governments in major ASEAN economies. ASEAN's share of regional sustainable bond issuance climbed to 8.0% in 2022 from 6.8% in 2021, higher than its share of 3.5% of general bond issuance in ASEAN+3.

ASEAN economies are active issuers of sustainability bonds in the region. ASEAN markets accounted for 30.1% of regional sustainability bond issuance in 2022, making the group the second-largest issuer of sustainability bonds in ASEAN+3 after the Republic of Korea, which accounted for 30.8% of regional sustainability bond issuance (**Figure 22**). The PRC remained the largest issuer of sustainable bonds in the region, accounting for a 52.0% share of the total, slightly lagging its 55.1% share of ASEAN+3's aggregate bond issuance in 2022. The PRC also led the region in the issuance of green bonds and sustainability-linked bonds in 2022, accounting for 70.8% and 62.9% of issuance, respectively. Japan, the second-largest sustainable bond issuer in 2022, dominated the issuance of transition bonds with 82.2% of the regional total. The Republic of Korea led the issuance of social bonds with a 57.0% share.

ASEAN+3's sustainable bond market is dominated by private sector issuance, suggesting there is great potential for more issuance from the public sector. In 2022, 76.8% of ASEAN+3's sustainable bond issuance originated in the private sector. This is in stark contrast to the private sector's 26.9% share of the region's overall bond issuance in 2022. This indicates there is great potential for the expansion of issuance in the public sector, including from municipals and state-owned entities. In ASEAN, the public sector accounted for 58.0% of sustainable bond issuance, driven by a few large sovereign issuances in 2022.

---

[9] ASEAN+3 is defined to include member states of the Association of Southeast Asian Nations (ASEAN) plus the People's Republic of China; Hong Kong, China; Japan; and the Republic of Korea.

Box 6: Link between Environmental, Social, and Governance Assets and Conventional Assets—Some Empirical Evidence

Sustainable assets are an emerging class of alternative assets.[a] For investors, these assets can potentially contribute to financial stability and portfolio diversification. Formally known as environmental, social, and governance (ESG) assets, this asset class has experienced rapid growth in recent years. Companies and industries are increasingly prioritizing sustainable practices in their business operations. The global financial crisis further catalyzed the growth of ESG investments. As a result, ESG has become an integral part of investment portfolios. Investors are turning away from investments in companies and industries that pursue environmentally harmful business practices. The growing awareness of sustainability investing among investors means that the growth of ESG assets is likely to continue. While such stylized facts are well known, what is largely lacking is a rigorous analysis of the contribution of ESG assets to systemic risk. This enables us to identify the systematic importance of such assets.

Issues related to ESG—such as environmental sustainability, climate change, business ethics, corporate governance, and human rights—are increasingly influencing the allocation of investments. Market players are reallocating their investments toward ESG assets from conventional assets. In the real economy, in response to growing concerns about the environment, energy producers are gravitating toward renewable energy and away from coal and hydrocarbons. By the same token, in financial markets, investors are gravitating from assets linked with conventional energy toward assets linked with cleaner energy. At a broader level, in recent years there has been a noticeable shift toward ESG assets in the portfolio management decisions of investors. The change in investor attitudes reflects a more general change in societal attitudes against unsustainable economic activities. The underlying goal of investors is to influence the behavior of firms and industries to promote better ESG outcomes.

Relative to conventional assets, ESG assets are characterized by more socially responsible investing, more ethical business practices, less environmental harm, and less leverage. Due to such characteristics, ESG assets tend to be more stable and less volatile than conventional assets. Another significant consideration is that large and growing ESG-related societal pressures are creating substantial risks, as evidenced by the increasing numbers of rules and regulations. Good ESG behavior by a firm reduces such risks, which in turn increases shareholder value. Therefore, it is in the self-interest of firms to avoid ESG risks and in the self-interest of investors to invest in ESG assets.

Although investment in ESG assets has grown rapidly, there are relatively few studies that rigorously analyze whether such investment actually benefits investors. In particular, there is only a thin literature on the impact of ESG investment in their main area of supposed benefit—i.e., risk mitigation and diversification of investment portfolios. Instead, existing studies mostly analyze the risk-adjusted returns of ESG assets versus conventional assets or the extent to which the two asset classes are linked with each other. A big shortcoming of the studies is that they do not examine the dynamics of how the link between ESG assets and conventional assets evolves over time.

Recent original research by Uddin et al. (2022) remedies the shortcoming in several ways. They empirically analyze the asymmetric effect of shocks to conventional assets on investments in nine major ESG assets. The analysis yields important implications on how investors can devise strategies to allocate their portfolios and manage their risks in the face of shocks. The analysis can also be useful for market regulators and policymakers. The main empirical methodology is the wavelet-based asymmetric copulas and systematic risk approach. A big advantage of this approach is that it allows for the analysis of effects at various time horizons. This matters because the investment horizon tends to differ for investors with different preferences. That is, the wavelet approach makes it possible to get a more dynamic and comprehensive understanding of the effect of shocks to conventional assets on ESG assets over time.

The analysis yields a number of interesting findings. The evidence points to a significant positive correlation between financial indices and most ESG assets. However, there is some evidence of negative connectedness between S&P green bonds and financial indices, which implies potential opportunities for portfolio diversification and risk management. The results also suggest that commodities and exchange rates present opportunities for ESG investors. Furthermore, gold is a potential safe haven for investors who purchase ESG assets. Overall, the findings generally suggest that a larger share of investments should be allocated to ESG assets relative to conventional assets to enhance portfolio diversification.

[a] This box was written by Donghyun Park (economic advisor) in the Economic Research and Regional Cooperation Department of the Asian Development Bank. This write-up is based on Uddin, Gazi Salah, Muhammad Yahya, Ali Ahmed, Donghyun Park, and Shu Tian. 2022. "In Search of Light in the Darkness: What We Learn from Ethical, Sustainable, and Green Investments." *International Journal of Finance and Economics*. 1–45. https://doi.org/10.1002/ijfe.2742.

Figure 19: Sustainable Bonds Outstanding in Global Markets

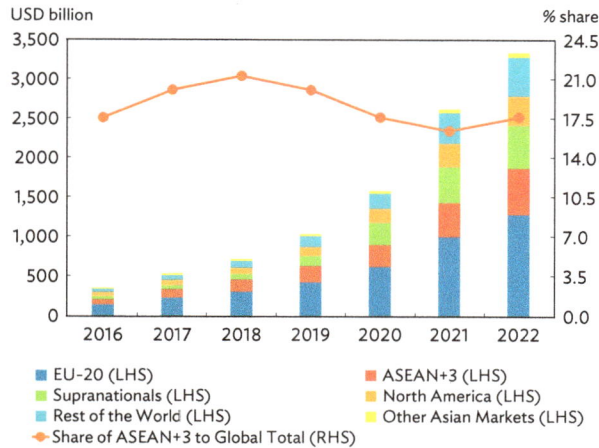

ASEAN+3 = Association of Southeast Asian Nations plus the People's Republic of China; Hong Kong, China; Japan; and the Republic of Korea, EU = European Union, LHS = left-hand side, RHS = right-hand side, USD = United States dollar.
Notes:
1. EU-20 includes EU member markets Austria, Belgium, Croatia, Cyprus, Estonia, Finland, France, Germany, Greece, Ireland, Italy, Latvia, Lithuania, Luxembourg, Malta, the Netherlands, Portugal, Slovakia, Slovenia, and Spain.
2. Data include both local currency and foreign currency issues.
Source: *AsianBondsOnline* computations based on Bloomberg LP data.

Figure 20: Market Profile of Outstanding ASEAN+3 Sustainable Bonds at the End of 2022

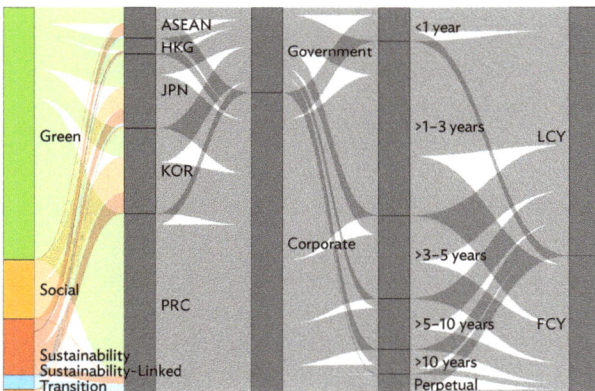

ASEAN = Association of Southeast Asian Nations; FCY = foreign currency; HKG = Hong Kong, China; JPN = Japan; KOR = Republic of Korea; LCY = local currency; PRC = People's Republic of China.
Note: ASEAN+3 is defined to include member states of the Association of Southeast Asian Nations (ASEAN) plus the People's Republic of China; Hong Kong, China; Japan; and the Republic of Korea.
Source: *AsianBondsOnline* computations based on Bloomberg LP data.

Sustainable bond issuance in the ASEAN+3 bond market remained concentrated in short- to medium-term tenors. The average size-weighted tenor of the region's sustainable bond issuances was 5.5 years in 2022, similar to the average of 5.6 years in 2021. Still, 78.9% of total issuances had maturities

Figure 21: ASEAN+3 Sustainable Bond Issuance in 2022 by Economy

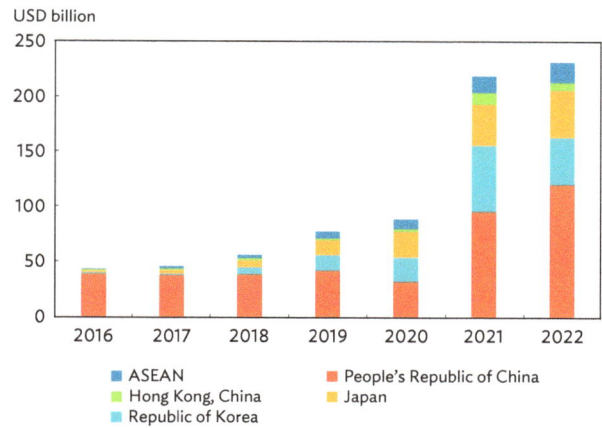

ASEAN = Association of Southeast Asian Nations; USD = United States dollar.
Note: ASEAN+3 is defined to include member states of the Association of Southeast Asian Nations (ASEAN) plus the People's Republic of China; Hong Kong, China; Japan; and the Republic of Korea.
Source: *AsianBondsOnline* computations based on Bloomberg LP data.

Figure 22: Market Profile of ASEAN+3 Sustainable Bond Issuance in 2022

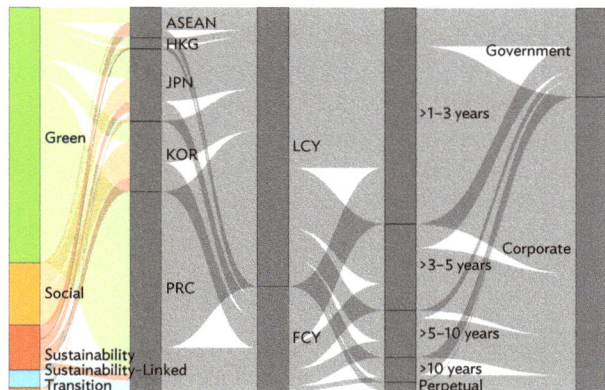

ASEAN = Association of Southeast Asian Nations; FCY = foreign currency; HKG = Hong Kong, China; JPN = Japan; KOR = Republic of Korea; LCY = local currency; PRC = People's Republic of China.
Note: ASEAN+3 is defined to include member states of the Association of Southeast Asian Nations (ASEAN) plus the People's Republic of China; Hong Kong, China; Japan; and the Republic of Korea.
Source: *AsianBondsOnline* computations based on Bloomberg LP data.

of less than 5 years, compared to 31.6% in the EU-20. LCY issuance accounted for 72.6% of ASEAN+3 sustainable bond issuance in 2022, which was lower than the LCY issuance share of 96.3% in ASEAN+3's overall bond market and the 88.0% share of LCY issuance in the EU-20's sustainable bond market in 2022. Among all bond types, sustainability bonds had the highest share of foreign-currency-denominated issuance in 2022.

Policy and Regulatory Developments

People's Republic of China

People's Bank of China Cuts Reserve Requirement Ratio

On 25 November, the People's Bank of China reduced the reserve requirement ratio for financial institutions by 25 basis points, effective 5 December. The central bank estimated that the move will release about CNY500 billion into the financial system.

Hong Kong, China

Hong Kong Monetary Authority Keeps Countercyclical Buffer Ratio at 1.0%

On 8 February, the Hong Kong Monetary Authority kept the countercyclical buffer ratio (CCyB) steady at 1.0%, noting that uncertainties in the global and domestic economic environment remain elevated despite initial signs of stabilization in the domestic economy. The Hong Kong Monetary Authority deemed that keeping the CCyB unchanged and monitoring the situation closely was appropriate amid lingering economic uncertainties. The CCyB is an integral part of the Basel III regulatory capital framework intended to improve the resilience of the banking sector in periods of excess credit growth.

Indonesia

Indonesian Parliament Approves Central Bank Bond Purchases in Times of Crisis

In December, the Indonesian Parliament approved into law the expanded mandate of Bank Indonesia to support the state budget during crisis periods. The law legalizes Bank Indonesia's government bond purchases, similar to what it has engaged in since 2020 when the coronavirus disease (COVID-19) pandemic started. At that time, however, an emergency regulation was adopted to allow the central bank to engage in bond purchases. Among the provisions of the new law, Bank Indonesia will be allowed to participate in government bond auctions in the primary market when a crisis has been announced by the government. The new legislation is part of the government's financial sector reform that aims to update past regulations and adapt to recent market developments.

Republic of Korea

The Republic of Korea Announces 2023 Economic Outlook and Policy Directions

On 21 December, the Government of the Republic of Korea announced its 2023 economic outlook along with its policy directions. Annual economic growth for 2023 is projected to be 1.6%, which is lower than the 2022 outlook due to deteriorating external conditions and a slowdown in consumption recovery due to rising interest rates. Consumer price inflation is projected to be 3.5% in 2023, which is also lower than the 5.1% outlook for 2022 amid a decline in global demand and raw material prices. The current account balance forecast for 2023 is USD21 billion, down from the 2022 outlook of USD22 billion, as the deficit in the services balance is expected to increase amid the resumption of overseas travel. Its 2023 policy directions include (i) managing the macroeconomy in a stable manner, (ii) supporting the recovery of people's livelihoods, (iii) boosting the economy by focusing on the private sector, and (iv) implementing structural reforms.

National Assembly Passes the 2023 Budget

On 23 December, the National Assembly of the Republic of Korea approved and passed the 2023 budget totaling KRW638.7 trillion, which is KRW0.3 trillion lower than the government's proposal of KRW639.0 trillion. The 2023 budget is also 5.1% higher than the original 2022 budget of KRW607.7 trillion, but it is 6.0% lower if including the supplementary budgets (KRW679.5 trillion) in 2022. Government revenues were also reduced by KRW0.3 trillion to KRW625.7 trillion. The managed and consolidated fiscal deficits were maintained at KRW58.2 trillion and KRW13.1 trillion, respectively, along with the consolidated fiscal deficit as a percentage of gross domestic product at 0.6%. Government debt was also lowered to KRW1,134.4 trillion from KRW1,134.8 trillion, but the resulting percentage of gross domestic product was kept at 49.8%.

Malaysia

Malaysia Signs Agreement with Other Central Banks on Payment Connectivity Cooperation

On 14 November, Bank Negara Malaysia—together with Bank Indonesia, Bangko Sentral ng Pilipinas, Monetary Authority of Singapore, and Bank of Thailand—signed a memorandum of understanding to cooperate in the regional payment connectivity initiative. The program aims to promote growth by enhancing intra-regional trade and investment through a harmonious financial ecosystem in the region. It also encourages small- and medium-sized enterprises to participate in the international market. Cooperation on regional payment connectivity will help fast-track the region's financial digitalization and reinforce the Association of Southeast Asian Nations' goal of having a connected payment system to make cross-border payments easier for member economies.

Philippines

The Philippines to Borrow PHP2.21 Trillion to Support Funding of 2023 State Budget

On 16 December, the Philippine president signed into law the 2023 General Appropriations Act authorizing a national budget of PHP5.27 trillion to support the government's 2023 economic agenda. The 2023 budget is 4.9% higher than the previous year's level of PHP5.02 trillion and will prioritize the education, infrastructure, health, agriculture, and social security sectors. To support financing of the national budget, the government plans to borrow PHP2.21 trillion in 2023. The planned borrowing will comprise 75% (PHP1.65 trillion) domestic debt and 25% (PHP553.50 billion) foreign borrowing. Domestic borrowing will be made through auctions of Treasury bills, notes, and bonds to the public, while foreign borrowing will be acquired through loans from foreign financial institutions or by floating government securities in the international market.

Singapore

Singapore and Japan Renew Currency Swap Agreement

On 29 November, the Monetary Authority of Singapore and the Bank of Japan renewed their bilateral local currency swap arrangement for another 3 years. The agreement allows the two central banks to swap up to SGD15.0 billion or JPY1.1 trillion, providing liquidity in Japanese yen to financial institutions in Singapore and Singapore dollar liquidity to entities in Japan. The agreement also helps facilitate intra-regional payments between the two economies.

Thailand

Bank of Thailand Announces End of Corporate Bond Stabilization Fund

On 31 October, the Bank of Thailand announced that it would end its temporary corporate bond support under the corporate bond stabilization fund after 31 December 2022. The fund was created in 2020 to help boost confidence in the corporate bond market and aid companies experiencing momentary liquidity problems amid the COVID-19 pandemic. The supervisory committee of the bond stabilization fund deemed that the need for support had lessened as the economy continued to recover.

Government Switches THB17.2 Billion of Short-Term Bonds

On 9 November, the Public Debt Management Office conducted bond-switching transactions amounting to THB17.2 billion. The transactions involved swapping bonds with a remaining maturity of 1.1 years to six destination bonds with remaining maturities ranging from 5.6 years to 49.6 years. The bond swap allowed the government to improve debt management by extending the repayment periods of the maturing bonds.

Viet Nam

State Bank of Vietnam Raises 2022 Credit Growth Cap of Domestic Banking System

On 5 December, the State Bank of Vietnam raised the local banking system's credit target by 1.5–2.0 percentage points from the previous 14%, following the central bank's policy rate increases that had caused a credit crunch in the domestic real estate and financial markets. Banks with good liquidity and low interest rate offerings are eligible for the credit cap increase. The new policy aims to balance appropriate capital to provide credit and focus capital on economic growth drivers such as production and business sectors. The State Bank of Vietnam recognizes the risks that come with credit expansion and will closely monitor developments in the international and domestic markets and take appropriate measures to ensure liquidity, operational safety, and solvency for market participants.

AsianBondsOnline Annual Bond Market Liquidity Survey

Introduction

AsianBondsOnline conducts a local currency (LCY) bond market survey every year to assess overall liquidity conditions in emerging East Asia.[10] The survey allows *AsianBondsOnline* to identify both short-term factors currently driving market liquidity and trading as well as structural factors that affect bond market liquidity in the longer run. The survey helps identify hindrances to the proper functioning of the region's LCY bond markets and assist policy makers and regulators to further develop regional LCY bond markets.

The 2022 liquidity survey was conducted online in December 2022 among a broad range of market participants including banks, market brokers, fund managers, investment companies, insurance companies, rating agencies, and bond pricing agencies. The survey consists of both a quantitative and qualitative assessment of the government and corporate LCY bond markets in emerging East Asia. Quantitative factors include metrics such as bid–ask spreads and transaction sizes, while the qualitative section attempts to assess structural factors and their corresponding degree of development. In addition, given increasing awareness and interest among investors and issuers in the sustainable finance market, the survey also includes a brief section on market interest in sustainable bonds to identify factors driving the trading of sustainable bonds.

Overall Liquidity Conditions

Overall liquidity conditions in emerging East Asian LCY bond markets weakened in 2022 from the previous year. As shown in **Figure 23**, nearly all Association of Southeast Asian Nations (ASEAN) markets and the Republic of Korea reported a decrease in overall liquidity, with 61.1% of respondents saying that liquidity decreased in 2022, compared with 36.4% noting decreased liquidity in 2021. This was largely due to tightening financial conditions in both global and domestic financial markets. In the international financial centers of Singapore and

Figure 23: Liquidity Conditions by Economy in Emerging East Asia

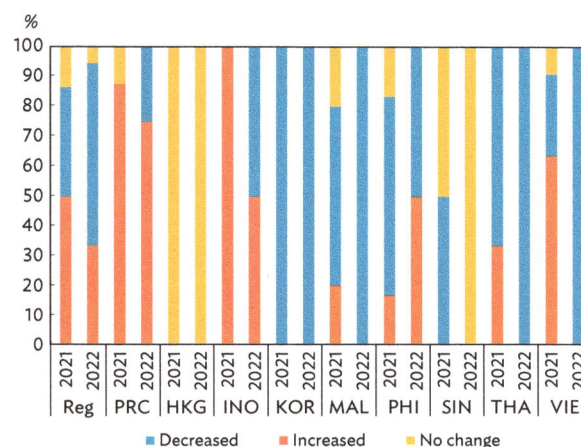

HKG = Hong Kong, China; INO = Indonesia; KOR = Republic of Korea; MAL = Malaysia; PHI = Philippines; PRC = People's Republic of China; Reg = Regional; SIN = Singapore; THA = Thailand; VIE = Viet Nam.
Source: *AsianBondsOnline* 2022 Local Currency Bond Market Liquidity Survey.

Hong Kong, China, survey participants observed that liquidity conditions remained unchanged from the prior year. In the People's Republic of China (PRC), which was the only emerging East Asian market that experienced monetary easing in 2022, more than 70% of survey participants noted an improvement in liquidity conditions in 2022.

Domestic and United States (US) monetary tightening were identified as the top two factors hampering market liquidity in 2022 (**Figure 24**). The region experienced an overall tightening of financial conditions in 2022, particularly during the second half of the year. Domestic monetary tightening was jointly driven by domestic inflationary pressures and measures to safeguard domestic financial stability amid aggressive monetary tightening in the US. Bond market liquidity was also significantly affected by market sentiment, which drives foreign portfolio investments and is very responsive to US monetary stances.

---

[10] In the context of the *AsianBondsOnline* 2022 Annual Bond Market Liquidity Survey, emerging East Asia comprises the People's Republic of China; Hong Kong, China; Indonesia; the Republic of Korea; Malaysia; the Philippines; Singapore; Thailand; and Viet Nam.

Figure 24: Factors Affecting Bond Market Liquidity in Emerging East Asia in 2022

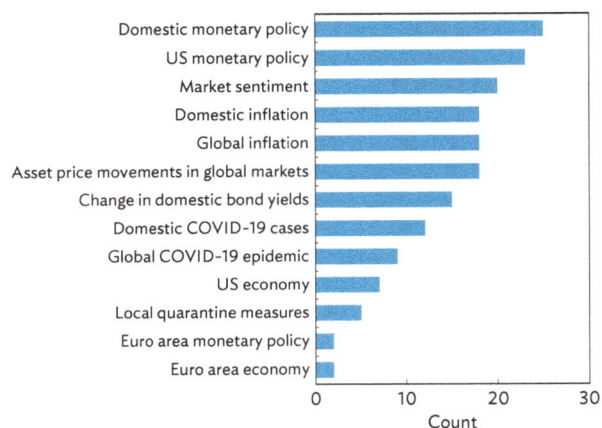

COVID-19 = coronavirus disease, US = United States.
Source: *AsianBondsOnline* 2022 Local Currency Bond Market Liquidity Survey.

Figure 25: Local Currency Government Bond Turnover Ratios in Select Emerging East Asian Markets

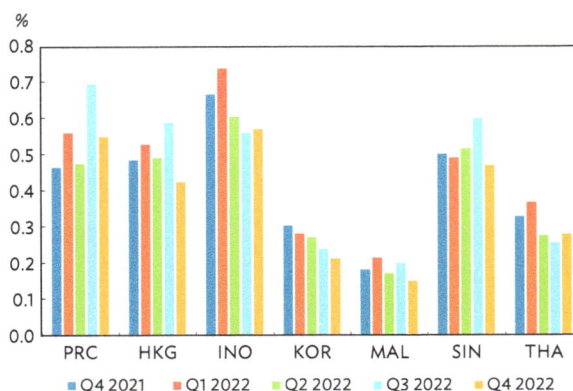

HKG = Hong Kong, China; INO = Indonesia; KOR = Republic of Korea; MAL = Malaysia; PRC = People's Republic of China; Q1 = first quarter; Q2 = second quarter; Q3 = third quarter; Q4 = fourth quarter; SIN = Singapore; THA = Thailand.

Note: Turnover ratios are calculated as local currency trading volume (sales amount only) divided by the average local currency value of outstanding bonds during each 3-month period.

Sources: People's Republic of China (CEIC Data Company); Hong Kong, China (Hong Kong Monetary Authority); Indonesia (Indonesia Stock Exchange); Republic of Korea (The Bank of Korea and KG Zeroin Corporation); Malaysia (Bank Negara Malaysia); Singapore (Monetary Authority of Singapore); and Thailand (Bank of Thailand and Thai Bond Market Association).

Government Bond Markets

Liquidity

The government bond turnover ratios in most ASEAN markets and the Republic of Korea trended down in much of 2022 amid tightening financial conditions. Consistent with Figure 23, such a declining trend was not that pronounced in financial centers like Singapore and Hong Kong, China, or in the PRC where an easing monetary stance was maintained (**Figure 25**). The People's Bank of China was not only the sole central bank in the region that lowered key reference rates in 2022, it also boosted liquidity through various fiscal measures such as tax cuts and rebates to support economic growth amid restrictive pandemic containment measures.

Bid–ask spreads widened in nearly all regional government bond markets in 2022 due to tightening financial conditions both internationally and domestically. Based on the survey, the region's average bid–ask spread for on-the-run and off-the-run government bonds, respectively, climbed to 8.1 basis points (bps) and 11.2 bps in 2022 from 3.1 bps and 4.8 bps in 2021 (**Figure 26** and **Figure 27**). Most markets saw widening bid–ask spreads in 2022 for both on-the-run and off-the-run government bonds amid tightened financial conditions. Despite continued easing measures in the

Figure 26: Average Bid–Ask Spreads for On-the-Run Government Bonds

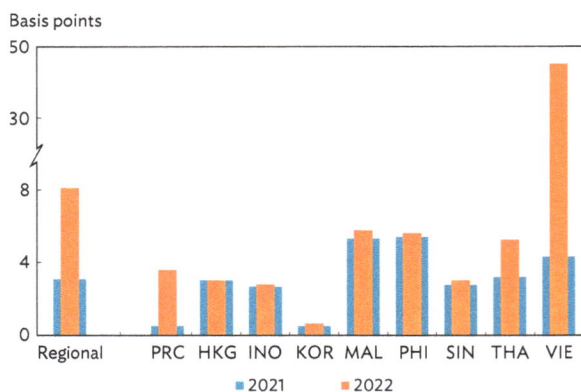

HKG = Hong Kong, China; INO = Indonesia; KOR = Republic of Korea; MAL = Malaysia; PHI = Philippines; PRC = People's Republic of China; SIN = Singapore; THA = Thailand; VIE = Viet Nam.

Note: The regional bid–ask spread refers to the average spread of the nine markets of emerging East Asia.

Source: *AsianBondsOnline* 2022 Local Currency Bond Market Liquidity Survey.

Figure 27: Average Bid–Ask Spreads for Off-the-Run Government Bonds

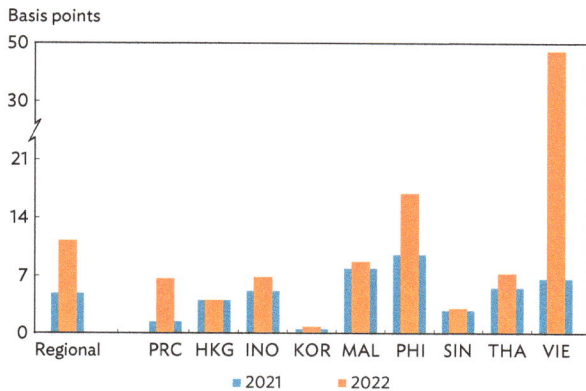

HKG = Hong Kong, China; INO = Indonesia; KOR = Republic of Korea; MAL = Malaysia; PHI = Philippines; PRC = People's Republic of China; SIN = Singapore; THA = Thailand; VIE = Viet Nam.
Note: The regional bid–ask spread refers to the average spread of the nine markets of emerging East Asia.
Source: *AsianBondsOnline* 2022 Local Currency Bond Market Liquidity Survey.

Figure 28: Typical Transaction Size for On-the-Run Government Bonds

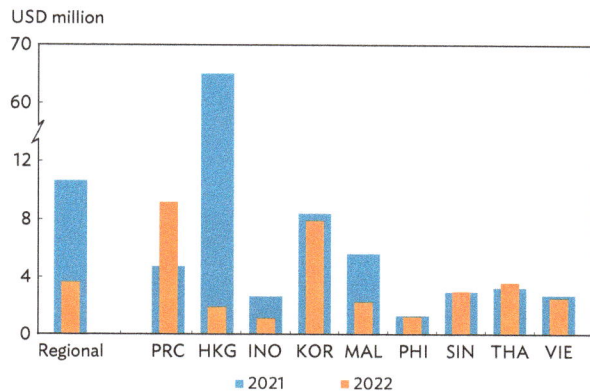

HKG = Hong Kong, China; INO = Indonesia; KOR = Republic of Korea; MAL = Malaysia; PHI = Philippines; PRC = People's Republic of China; SIN = Singapore; THA = Thailand; USD = United States dollar; VIE = Viet Nam.
Note: The regional transaction size refers to the average transaction size of the nine markets of emerging East Asia.
Source: *AsianBondsOnline* 2022 Local Currency Bond Market Liquidity Survey.

PRC, the bid–ask spread for government bonds rose on concerns over the prolonged impacts of its pandemic containment measures. On top of that, the continued easing led to widened interest rate differentials between the PRC and other global and regional markets, making its bonds less attractive to international investors.

Amid tightened liquidity conditions, the typical transaction size for government bonds declined in most emerging East Asian markets. The region's average transaction size for on-the-run government bonds fell to USD3.6 million in the 2022 survey from USD10.6 million in 2021 (**Figure 28**). In most markets, a smaller transaction size was recorded in 2022 than in the previous year.

Market Development

The results of the 2022 survey indicated a slight weakening of the regional bond market's structural environment. The survey includes participants' qualitative assessments of the development of the region's government bond markets based on a set of key structural factors. The regional averages for six of the eight structural factors from the 2022 survey were marginally lower than the corresponding regional averages from the 2021 survey (**Figure 29**).

Figure 29: Local Currency Government Bond Market Structural Issues in Emerging East Asia

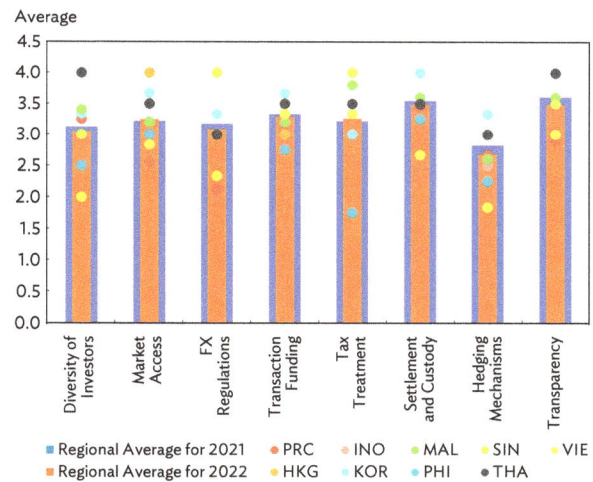

FX = foreign exchange; HKG = Hong Kong, China; INO = Indonesia; KOR = Republic of Korea; MAL = Malaysia; PHI = Philippines; PRC = People's Republic of China; SIN = Singapore; THA = Thailand; VIE = Viet Nam.
Source: *AsianBondsOnline* 2022 Local Currency Bond Market Liquidity Survey.

The most developed structural factors in the region's government bond markets are transparency and settlement and custody. Government bond market information remains widely available across the region. Most markets have official online platforms that provide data on bond market activities such as auction results. All markets except for Viet Nam received a score above 3.0 for settlement and custody, indicating the presence of systems that allow the efficient settlement of bond market transactions.

Transaction funding, tax treatment, and market access are fairly developed in the region. The average score for transaction funding was unchanged from the previous year at 3.3, indicating the continued availability of diverse funding sources in the region's government bond market. The average rating for tax treatment increased from 3.2 in 2021 to 3.3 in 2022. The Republic of Korea recorded a higher rating of 3.0 in 2022 compared with 2.7 in the previous year, as it removed taxes on foreign investors' income from government bonds in October 2022 to promote capital flows into the local bond market. In Singapore and Hong Kong, China, interest income from government bonds is tax-exempt. The region's average rating for market access increased to 3.3 in 2022 from 3.2 in the previous year. Hong Kong, China continued to have the region's highest score for market access at 4.0.

The rating for foreign exchange regulations fell in 2022, while the score for diversity of investors was unchanged. Financial centers like Singapore and Hong Kong, China had the highest ratings of 4.0 for foreign exchange regulations, while relatively closed markets like Viet Nam (2.3) and the PRC (2.1) had the lowest scores. Thailand relaxed its rules on foreign exchange transactions in April 2022, while the PRC announced new rules relaxing restrictions on foreign exchange transactions effective January 2023. For diversity of investors, all markets had scores above 3.0 except for the smaller markets of the Philippines (2.5) and Viet Nam (2.0).

Hedging mechanisms remain the area where further development is needed. The average rating for hedging mechanisms, the lowest among all structural factors, declined to 2.7 in 2022 from 2.8 in the prior year. This indicates the limited availability of mechanisms to guard against bond market risks in the region. More than half of the markets had scores below 3.0, reflecting the need for more hedging products in the region's bond

markets. Initiatives such as the planned "Swap Connect" between the PRC and Hong Kong, China, which will take effect in 2023, will provide additional hedging mechanisms for bond investors in the future.

Corporate Bond Markets

Liquidity

Emerging East Asia's corporate bond market remains less liquid than the government bond market as most investors in corporate bonds continue to buy and hold until maturity. Survey results showed that more respondents noted the absence of an active secondary market for corporate bonds this year (36%) than in 2021 (15%) (**Figure 30**).

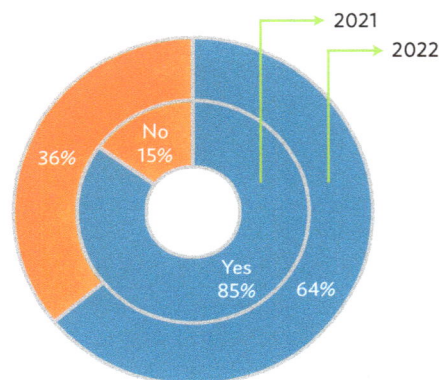

Figure 30: Is There an Active Secondary Bond Market for Corporate Bonds?

Note: Percentages refer to the share of survey respondents answering either "yes" or "no."
Source: *AsianBondsOnline* 2022 Local Currency Bond Market Liquidity Survey.

Widening bid–ask spreads in almost all regional markets reflect decreased liquidity in corporate bond markets in emerging East Asia. For the 2022 survey, the average bid–ask spread for the region grew to 22.6 bps from 16.3 bps in 2021 (**Figure 31**). Only the PRC registered a lower bid–ask spread of 4.9 bps, compared with 5.3 bps in 2021, as the PRC sought to support economic activities through loose fiscal and monetary policies. Viet Nam and the Philippines witnessed larger increases in their respective corporate bid–ask spreads. Their corporate bond markets are relatively less developed than those of their ASEAN peers, and investors in the corporate

Figure 31: Average Bid–Ask Spreads for Corporate Bonds

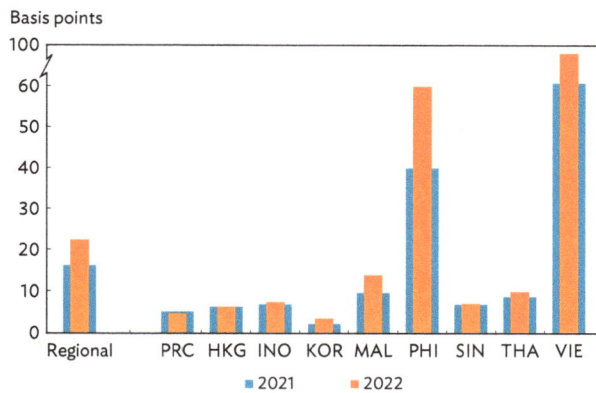

HKG = Hong Kong, China; INO = Indonesia; KOR = Republic of Korea;
MAL = Malaysia; PHI = Philippines; PRC = People's Republic of China;
SIN = Singapore; THA = Thailand; VIE = Viet Nam.
Notes:
1. The regional bid–ask spread refers to the average spread of the nine markets of
   emerging East Asia.
2. For the Philippines and Viet Nam, the bid–ask spreads quoted are for a newly
   issued corporate bonds.
Source: *AsianBondsOnline* 2022 Local Currency Bond Market Liquidity Survey.

Figure 32: Average Transaction Sizes for Corporate Bonds

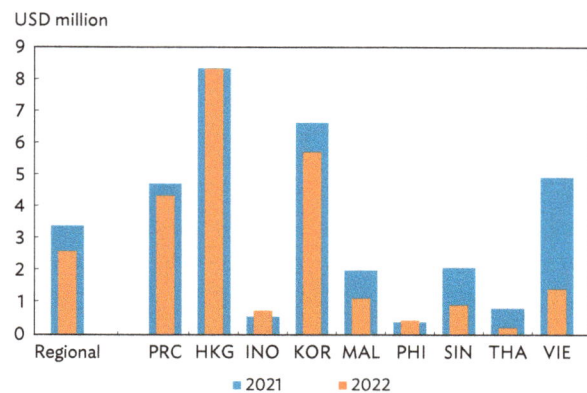

HKG = Hong Kong, China; INO = Indonesia; KOR = Republic of Korea;
MAL = Malaysia; PHI = Philippines; PRC = People's Republic of China;
SIN = Singapore; THA = Thailand; USD = United States dollar; VIE = Viet Nam.
Note: The regional transaction size refers to the average transaction size of the nine
markets of emerging East Asia.
Source: *AsianBondsOnline* 2022 Local Currency Bond Market Liquidity Survey.

bonds of Viet Nam and the Philippines tend to hold their fixed-income securities to maturity. Also, the quoted bid–ask spreads for both markets refer to newly issued bonds, as most participants noted an absence of an active secondary market for corporate bonds.

The average transaction size for the region's corporate bond market declined to USD2.6 million in 2022 from USD3.4 million in the previous year. Most markets in the region recorded a smaller average transaction size in 2022 (**Figure 32**). The largest contraction in average corporate bond market transaction size was recorded in Viet Nam where the mean transaction size dropped to USD1.4 million from USD4.9 million in 2021. Turnover ratios for corporate bonds declined between the fourth quarter of 2021 and the fourth quarter of 2022 in most emerging East Asian markets for which data are available. The PRC's turnover ratio rose significantly in the final quarter of 2022 when pandemic containment measures were lifted (**Figure 33**).

Figure 33: Local Currency Corporate Bond Turnover Ratios

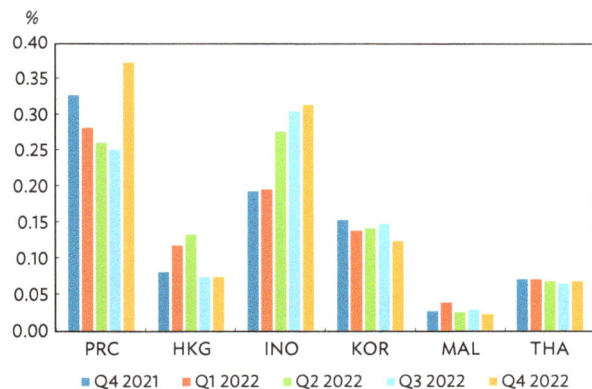

HKG = Hong Kong, China; INO = Indonesia; KOR = Republic of Korea;
MAL = Malaysia; PRC = People's Republic of China; Q1 = first quarter;
Q2 = second quarter; Q3 = third quarter; Q4 = fourth quarter; THA = Thailand.
Note: Turnover ratios are calculated as local currency trading volume (sales
amount only) divided by average local currency value of outstanding bonds
during each 3-month period.
Sources: People's Republic of China (CEIC Data Company); Hong Kong, China
(Hong Kong Monetary Authority); Indonesia (Indonesia Stock Exchange); Republic
of Korea (The Bank of Korea and KG Zeroin Corporation); Malaysia (Bank Negara
Malaysia); and Thailand (Bank of Thailand and Thai Bond Market Association).

Market Development

The results of the 2022 liquidity survey on key structural factors in emerging East Asia's corporate bond markets were largely the same as in 2021.
The 2022 survey showed that most structural factors scored an average of 3.0 or above and that regional corporate bond markets' diversity of the investor profile and hedging mechanisms are areas that need further improvements (**Figure 34**). Transaction funding in the corporate bond markets of emerging East Asia had an average score of 3.4, while a regional average of 3.2 was recorded for settlement and custody. Market access, tax treatment, and transparency each reported a regional average rating of 3.0. Compared to the 2021 survey results, tax treatment marginally improved, reaching an average score of 3.0 from 2.9. Survey participants continued to express their desire for a more diverse investor profile in the corporate bond markets of emerging East Asia. Similar to 2021, the market structure category that recorded the lowest average score in the region in 2022 was hedging mechanisms, with an average of 2.2. Proper risk management tools continued to elude almost all markets in emerging East Asia.

Sustainable Bond Markets

For the 2022 *AsianBondsOnline* liquidity survey, participants were queried to assess their level of interest in investments in sustainable bonds as well as the corresponding motivations or lack thereof. The goal is to guide policymakers and regulators in their creation of environmental, social, and governance (ESG) frameworks and initiatives to promote ESG investing.

There is a high level of investment interest in sustainable bonds in emerging East Asia, but in some markets investor education is still needed to boost awareness and interest. In 2022, 80% of participants in the region said that they or their organization have plans for trading and investing in sustainable bonds (**Figure 35**). Among these respondents, the most cited driving factor was portfolio diversification, followed by their respective organization's inclusion of ESG criteria and mounting market interest (**Figure 36, Panel A**). This suggests that investors are becoming increasingly conscious of the importance of ESG investing and are applying ESG criteria in their investments. Among participants who stated they had no plans for trading and investing in sustainable bonds, a lack of market interest was cited as the biggest reason, followed by their respective firms having not yet adopted ESG criteria

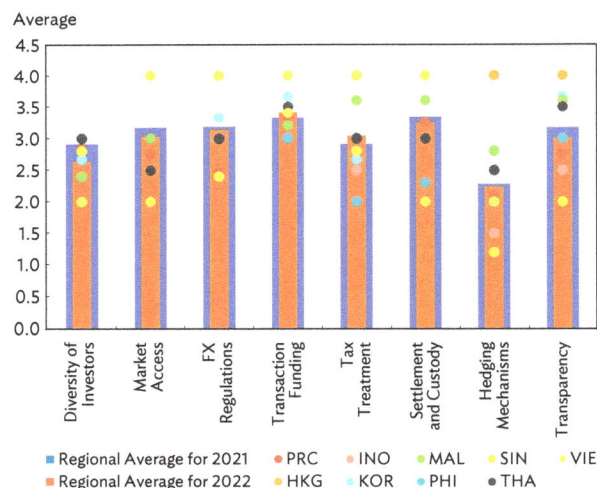

Figure 34: Local Currency Corporate Bond Market Structural Issues in Emerging East Asia

FX = foreign exchange; HKG = Hong Kong, China; INO = Indonesia; KOR = Republic of Korea; MAL = Malaysia; PHI = Philippines; PRC = People's Republic of China; SIN = Singapore; THA = Thailand; VIE = Viet Nam.
Source: *AsianBondsOnline* 2022 Local Currency Bond Market Liquidity Survey.

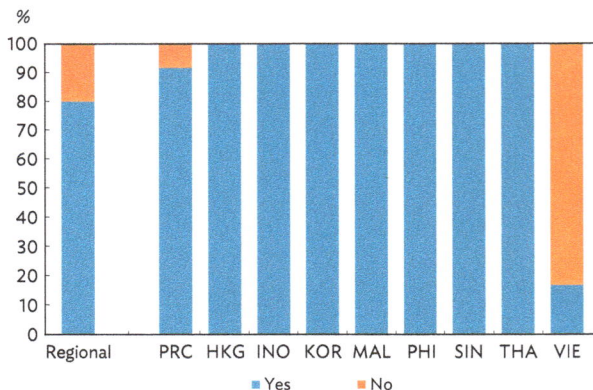

Figure 35: Interest in Trading Sustainable Bonds across Markets

HKG = Hong Kong, China; INO = Indonesia; KOR = Republic of Korea; MAL = Malaysia; PHI = Philippines; PRC = People's Republic of China; SIN = Singapore; THA = Thailand; VIE = Viet Nam.
Source: *AsianBondsOnline* 2022 Local Currency Bond Market Liquidity Survey.

Figure 36: Factors Affecting Sustainable Bond Investment

Panel A. Participants who answered "Yes" to investing in ESG

Panel B. Participants who answered "No" to investing in ESG

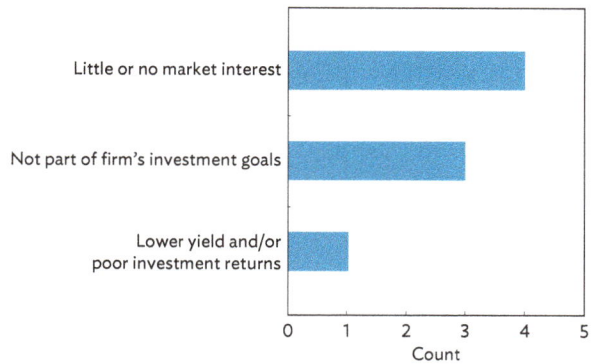

ESG = environmental, social, and governance.
Source: *AsianBondsOnline* 2022 Local Currency Bond Market Liquidity Survey.

as part of their investment goals (**Figure 36, Panel B**). This suggests that promoting investor education and raising market awareness of the importance and benefits of ESG investing could be a viable strategy for improving investor interest.

When asked about liquidity, 54.2% of participants said that sustainable bond market liquidity was roughly comparable to that of conventional bond markets. However, 33.3% observed that ESG bonds were less liquid than conventional bonds (**Figure 37**). Considering the relatively smaller size of sustainable bond markets compared to conventional bond markets, and the fact that corporate bonds dominate sustainable bond markets in the region, the liquidity conditions of the region's sustainable bond markets are considered acceptable.

Figure 37: Sustainable Bond Market Liquidity

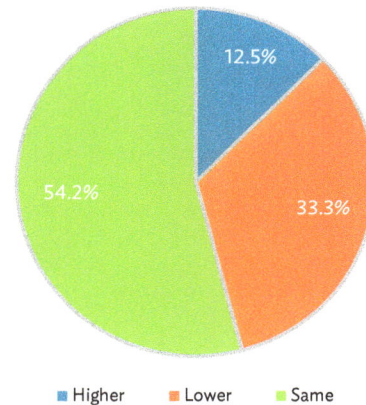

Source: *AsianBondsOnline* 2022 Local Currency Bond Market Liquidity Survey.

Market Summaries

People's Republic of China

The People's Republic of China's (PRC) local currency (LCY) bonds outstanding rose 1.3% quarter-on-quarter (q-o-q) and 10.6% year-on-year to CNY127.4 trillion (USD18.5 trillion) at the end of the fourth quarter (Q4) of 2022. Q-o-q growth moderated from 2.2% in the previous quarter as growth in government bonds slowed on declining local government bond issuance and corporate bonds outstanding contracted on economic uncertainty.

Table 1: Size and Composition of the Local Currency Bond Market in the People's Republic of China

| | Outstanding Amount (billion) | | | | | | Growth Rates (%) | | | |
| | Q4 2021 | | Q3 2022 | | Q4 2022 | | Q4 2021 | | Q4 2022 | |
	CNY	USD	CNY	USD	CNY	USD	q-o-q	y-o-y	q-o-q	y-o-y
Total	115,154	18,117	125,779	17,676	127,367	18,463	3.9	13.6	1.3	10.6
Government	74,373	11,701	81,918	11,512	83,643	12,125	4.5	14.2	2.1	12.5
Treasury Bonds	23,420	3,685	25,261	3,550	26,152	3,791	4.7	11.9	3.5	11.7
Central Bank Bonds	15	2	15	2	15	2	0.0	0.0	0.0	0.0
Policy Bank Bonds	19,681	3,096	20,984	2,949	21,427	3,106	2.2	9.1	2.1	8.9
Local Government Bonds	31,257	4,918	35,658	5,011	36,049	5,226	5.8	19.6	1.1	15.3
Corporate	40,781	6,416	43,861	6,164	43,724	6,338	2.9	12.4	(0.3)	7.2

( ) = negative, CNY = Chinese yuan, q-o-q = quarter-on-quarter, Q3 = third quarter, Q4 = fourth quarter, USD = United States dollar, y-o-y = year-on-year.

Notes:
1. Treasury bonds include savings bonds and local government bonds.
2. Bloomberg LP end-of-period local currency–USD rates are used.
3. Growth rates are calculated from a local currency base and do not include currency effects.

Sources: CEIC and Bloomberg LP.

Total LCY corporate bond issuance in the PRC fell 6.5% q-o-q to CNY4.3 trillion in Q4 2022. On a year-on-year basis, LCY corporate bond issuance dropped 18.7% amid economic uncertainty. The top issuances in Q4 2022 were mostly from banks as they issued subordinated bonds to help shore up their capital.

Table 2: Notable Local Currency Corporate Bond Issuances in the Fourth Quarter of 2022

Corporate Issuers	Coupon Rate (%)	Issued Amount (CNY billion)	Corporate Issuers	Coupon Rate (%)	Issued Amount (CNY billion)
China State Railway Group[a]			Bank of Communications[a]		
5-year bond	2.76	20	3-year bond	2.98	30
10-year bond	3.02	12	3-year bond	2.96	10
10-year bond	3.28	10	10-year bond	3.03	37
10-year bond	3.27	10	15-year bond	3.36	13
10-year bond	3.50	10	China Reform Holdings[a]		
10-year bond	2.99	10	3-year bond	2.59	3
20-year bond	3.22	10	5-year bond	2.85	20
30-year bond	3.76	10	5-year bond	2.85	20
30-year bond	3.47	10	5-year bond	2.85	10
30-year bond	3.42	10	Industrial and Commercial Bank of China[a]		
30-year bond	3.30	8	10-year bond	3.70	25
Bank of China[a]			10-year bond	3.00	5
3-year bond	2.92	30	15-year bond	3.34	10
10-year bond	3.02	50	15-year bond	3.85	5
15-year bond	3.34	15			

CNY = Chinese yuan.

[a] Multiple issuance of the same tenor indicates issuance on different dates.

Source: Bloomberg LP.

By the end of 2022, the corporate bonds outstanding of the top 30 corporate issuers reached CNY11.2 trillion, comprising 25.6% of the total market. China State Railway Group remained the dominant issuer with outstanding bonds of CNY1.8 trillion, more than double that of the second-largest issuer, Bank of China, which had CNY0.9 trillion worth of bonds outstanding.

Table 3: Top 30 Issuers of Local Currency Corporate Bonds in the People's Republic of China

	Issuers	Outstanding Amount		State-Owned	Listed Company	Type of Industry
		LCY Bonds (CNY billion)	LCY Bonds (USD billion)			
1.	China State Railway Group	1,823.5	264.3	Yes	No	Transportation
2.	Bank of China	905.0	131.2	Yes	Yes	Banking
3.	Industrial and Commercial Bank of China	883.0	128.0	Yes	Yes	Banking
4.	Agricultural Bank of China	830.0	120.3	Yes	Yes	Banking
5.	China Construction Bank	613.0	88.9	Yes	Yes	Banking
6.	Bank of Communications	569.5	82.6	Yes	Yes	Banking
7.	Shanghai Pudong Development Bank	540.2	78.3	Yes	Yes	Banking
8.	Industrial Bank	407.6	59.1	No	Yes	Banking
9.	Central Huijin Investment	370.0	53.6	Yes	No	Asset Management
10.	China Citic Bank	355.0	51.5	No	No	Banking
11.	State Grid Corporation of China	340.0	49.3	Yes	No	Energy
12.	China Everbright Bank	302.3	43.8	No	Yes	Banking
13.	China Minsheng Bank	265.3	38.4	No	Yes	Banking
14.	Huaxia Bank	250.0	36.2	No	Yes	Banking
15.	State Power Investment	248.3	36.0	Yes	No	Power
16.	Postal Savings Bank of China	240.0	34.8	Yes	Yes	Banking
17.	Ping An Bank	230.0	33.3	No	Yes	Banking
18.	China Merchants Bank	206.1	29.9	No	Yes	Banking
19.	China National Petroleum	164.3	23.8	Yes	No	Power
20.	Bank of Beijing	163.9	23.8	No	Yes	Banking
21.	China Merchants Securities	160.0	23.2	Yes	Yes	Brokerage
22.	Tianjin Infrastructure Investment Group	155.9	22.6	Yes	No	Holding Firm
23.	Shaanxi Coal and Chemical Industry Group	151.0	21.9	Yes	Yes	Coal
24.	China Southern Power Grid	150.0	21.7	No	Yes	Energy
25.	China Reform Holdings	148.8	21.6	Yes	No	Holding Firm
26.	Huatai Securities	145.3	21.1	No	Yes	Brokerage
27.	Bank of Shanghai	142.6	20.7	Yes	Yes	Banking
28.	GF Securities	139.7	20.3	No	Yes	Brokerage
29.	China Galaxy Securities	137.1	19.9	no	Yes	Brokerage
30.	China Cinda Asset Management	135.0	19.6	Yes	Yes	Holding Firm
Total Top 30 LCY Corporate Issuers		**11,172.4**	**1,619.5**			
Total LCY Corporate Bonds		**43,724.0**	**6,338.1**			
Top 30 as % of Total LCY Corporate Bonds		**25.6%**	**25.6%**			

CNY = Chinese yuan, LCY = local currency, USD = United States dollar.
Notes:
1. Data as of 31 December 2022.
2. State-owned firms are defined as those in which the government has more than a 50% ownership stake.
Source: *AsianBondsOnline* calculations based on Bloomberg LP data.

Hong Kong, China

Hong Kong, China's local currency (LCY) bond market reached a size of HKD2,770.5 billion (USD355.1 billion) at the end of the fourth quarter (Q4) of 2022. Overall growth slowed to 0.8% quarter-on-quarter (q-o-q) in Q4 2022 from 4.9% q-o-q in the third quarter as expansion in both the government and corporate bond segments moderated. On a year-on-year basis, growth eased to 9.7% in Q4 2022 from 13.2% in the previous quarter.

Table 1: Size and Composition of the Local Currency Bond Market in Hong Kong, China

| | Outstanding Amount (billion) | | | | | | Growth Rate (%) | | | |
| | Q4 2021 | | Q3 2022 | | Q4 2022 | | Q4 2021 | | Q4 2022 | |
	HKD	USD	HKD	USD	HKD	USD	q-o-q	y-o-y	q-o-q	y-o-y
Total	2,525	324	2,748	350	2,770	355	4.0	5.0	0.8	9.7
Government	1,317	169	1,433	183	1,446	185	5.2	11.2	0.9	9.8
Exchange Fund Bills	1,125	144	1,174	150	1,186	152	5.7	7.9	1.0	5.4
Exchange Fund Notes	23	3	22	3	21	3	(3.3)	(6.4)	(3.6)	(9.4)
HKSAR Bonds	168	22	236	30	239	31	2.7	44.4	0.9	41.9
Corporate	1,208	155	1,315	168	1,324	170	2.7	(1.0)	0.7	9.6

( ) = negative, HKD = Hong Kong dollar, HKSAR = Hong Kong Special Administrative Region, q-o-q = quarter-on-quarter, Q3 = third quarter, Q4 = fourth quarter, USD = United States dollar, y-o-y = year-on-year.
Notes:
1. Bloomberg LP end-of-period local currency–USD rates are used.
2. Growth rates are calculated from a local currency base and do not include currency effects.
Source: Hong Kong Monetary Authority.

Issuance of LCY corporate bonds amounted to HKD194.1 billion in Q4 2022, down 19.7% q-o-q from HKD241.6 billion in the preceding quarter amid tighter liquidity conditions. Sustained monetary policy tightening by the United States Federal Reserve continued to affect Hong Kong, China's financial market due to the Hong Kong dollar's peg to the United States dollar. Among the notable issuances in Q4 2022 was Hong Kong Mortgage Corporation's inaugural social bond, a dual-currency issuance that included an HKD8.0 billion 2-year bond.[11]

Table 2: Notable Local Currency Corporate Bond Issuances in the Fourth Quarter of 2022

Corporate Issuers	Coupon Rate (%)	Issued Amount (HKD billion)	Corporate Issuers	Coupon Rate (%)	Issued Amount (HKD billion)
Hong Kong Mortgage Corporation			MTR		
0.5-year bond	4.83	1.0	1-year bond	5.08	1.0
1-year bond	5.25	0.6	2-year bond	4.85	0.7
2-year social bond	5.00	8.0	3-year bond	5.10	0.5
3-year bond	5.06	0.3	AIA Group		
Link Holdings			3-year bond	5.04	1.2
5-year bond	4.50	3.3	The Hong Kong and China Gas Company		
			2-year bond	4.05	0.3
			3-year bond	4.82	0.4

HKD = Hong Kong dollar.
Source: Bloomberg LP.

---

[11] The issuance also included a CNY3.0 billion 3-year bond tranche.

The outstanding bonds of the top 30 nonbank corporate issuers in Hong Kong, China totaled HKD323.5 billion at the end of December, representing a 24.4% share of the LCY corporate bond market. With an outstanding bond stock of HKD92.6 billion, state-owned Hong Kong Mortgage Corporation remained the top issuer. Finance, real estate, and transportation companies dominated the top 30 list.

Table 3: Top 30 Nonbank Issuers of Local Currency Corporate Bonds in Hong Kong, China

	Issuers	Outstanding Amount		State-Owned	Listed Company	Type of Industry
		LCY Bonds (HKD billion)	LCY Bonds (USD billion)			
1.	Hong Kong Mortgage Corporation	92.6	11.9	Yes	No	Finance
2.	Sun Hung Kai & Co.	19.8	2.5	No	Yes	Finance
3.	The Hong Kong and China Gas Company	19.3	2.5	No	Yes	Utilities
4.	MTR	16.4	2.1	Yes	Yes	Transportation
5.	New World Development	15.3	2.0	No	Yes	Diversified
6.	Airport Authority	15.2	2.0	Yes	No	Transportation
7.	Henderson Land Development	14.2	1.8	No	Yes	Real Estate
8.	Hang Lung Properties	12.5	1.6	No	Yes	Real Estate
9.	Link Holdings	11.9	1.5	No	Yes	Finance
10.	Hongkong Land	11.5	1.5	No	No	Real Estate
11.	Wharf Real Estate Investment Company	11.2	1.4	No	Yes	Finance
12.	AIA Group	8.8	1.1	No	Yes	Insurance
13.	CK Asset Holdings	8.5	1.1	No	Yes	Real Estate
14.	Hongkong Electric	8.5	1.1	No	No	Utilities
15.	Swire Pacific	8.2	1.1	No	Yes	Diversified
16.	Cathay Pacific	7.6	1.0	No	Yes	Transportation
17.	Swire Properties	7.3	0.9	No	Yes	Diversified
18.	CLP Power Hong Kong Financing	6.6	0.8	No	No	Finance
19.	Hysan Development Corporation	5.7	0.7	No	Yes	Real Estate
20.	Lerthai Group	3.0	0.4	No	Yes	Real Estate
21.	Haitong International	2.8	0.4	No	Yes	Finance
22.	Wheelock and Company	2.8	0.4	No	Yes	Real Estate
23.	Ev Dynamics Holdings	2.4	0.3	No	Yes	Diversified
24.	South Shore Holdings	2.2	0.3	No	Yes	Industrial
25.	Future Days	2.2	0.3	No	No	Transportation
26.	IFC Development	2.0	0.3	No	No	Finance
27.	Champion REIT	1.7	0.2	No	Yes	Real Estate
28.	Asia Standard Hotel Group	1.2	0.2	No	Yes	Finance
29.	Yuexiu REIT	1.1	0.1	No	Yes	Real Estate
30.	Urban Renewal Authority	1.1	0.1	Yes	No	Industrial Services
	Total Top 30 Nonbank LCY Corporate Issuers	323.5	41.5			
	Total LCY Corporate Bonds	1,324.4	169.8			
	Top 30 as % of Total LCY Corporate Bonds	24.4%	24.4%			

HKD = Hong Kong dollar, LCY = local currency, REIT = real estate investment trust, USD = United States dollar.
Notes:
1. Data as of 31 December 2022.
2. State-owned firms are defined as those in which the government has more than a 50% ownership stake.
Source: AsianBondsOnline calculations based on Bloomberg LP data.

Indonesia

Indonesia's local currency bond market reached a size of USD5,950.8 trillion (USD382.2 billion) at the end of December with growth moderating in the fourth quarter (Q4) of 2022 on both a quarter-on-quarter and year-on-year basis. Growth in central government bonds eased as the government had mostly fulfilled its borrowing requirements for the year. The corporate bond segment contracted in Q4 2022 on tapered issuance amid rising borrowing costs as Bank Indonesia raised policy rates each month from August to December.

Table 1: Size and Composition of the Local Currency Bond Market in Indonesia

| | Outstanding Amount (billion) | | | | | | Growth Rate (%) | | | |
| | Q4 2021 | | Q3 2022 | | Q4 2022 | | Q4 2021 | | Q4 2022 | |
	IDR	USD	IDR	USD	IDR	USD	q-o-q	y-o-y	q-o-q	y-o-y
Total	5,314,547	373	5,747,003	377	5,950,757	382	4.4	17.7	3.5	12.0
Government	4,884,206	343	5,289,492	347	5,505,487	354	4.6	19.4	4.1	12.7
Central Govt. Bonds	4,678,977	328	5,101,614	335	5,309,430	341	4.9	20.9	4.1	13.5
of which: *sukuk*	841,973	59	961,761	63	980,189	63	0.9	22.6	1.9	16.4
Nontradable Bonds	143,892	10	141,668	9	142,934	9	(1.7)	(13.0)	0.9	(0.7)
of which: *sukuk*	31,666	2	26,412	2	31,054	2	1.6	(18.3)	17.6	(1.9)
Central Bank Bonds	61,337	4	46,209	3	53,123	3	1.0	10.7	15.0	(13.4)
of which: *sukuk*	61,337	4	46,209	3	53,123	3	1.0	10.7	15.0	(13.4)
Corporate	430,341	30	457,511	30	445,270	29	2.0	1.1	(2.7)	3.5
of which: *sukuk*	34,813	2	39,660	3	41,898	3	(3.7)	14.7	5.6	20.4

( ) = negative, IDR = Indonesian rupiah, q-o-q = quarter-on-quarter, Q3 = third quarter, Q4 = fourth quarter, USD = United States dollar, y-o-y = year-on-year.
Notes:
1. Bloomberg LP end-of-period local currency–USD rates are used.
2. Growth rates are calculated from a local currency base and do not include currency effects.
3. *Sukuk* refers to Islamic bonds.
Sources: Bank Indonesia; Directorate General of Budget Financing and Risk Management, Ministry of Finance; Indonesia Stock Exchange; and Bloomberg LP.

Higher borrowing costs curtailed issuance of local currency corporate bonds in Q4 2022, with total bond sales of IDR27.0 trillion. This represented a contraction of 51.7% quarter-on-quarter and 13.6% year-on-year. Leading the list of new bond issuances during the quarter was Indah Kiat Pulp & Paper, which issued an aggregate IDR5.3 trillion by tapping the debt market twice (October and December), similar with Q4 2021.

Table 2: Notable Local Currency Corporate Bond Issuances in the Fourth Quarter of 2022

Corporate Issuers	Coupon Rate (%)	Issued Amount (IDR billion)	Corporate Issuers	Coupon Rate (%)	Issued Amount (IDR billion)
Indah Kiat Pulp & Paper[a]			Sarana Multi Infrastruktur		
370-day bond	6.00	905	3-year bond	6.98	3,536
370-day bond	7.00	399	Merdeka Copper Gold		
370-day *sukuk mudharabah*	6.00	481	5-year bond	10.30	3,101
370-day *sukuk mudharabah*	7.00	186	OKI Pulp & Paper Mills		
3-year bond	9.75	1,604	370-day bond	6.75	306
3-year bond	10.50	625	370-day *sukuk mudharabah*	6.75	627
3-year *sukuk mudharabah*	9.75	455	3-year bond	10.50	1,743
3-year *sukuk mudharabah*	10.50	127	3-year *sukuk mudharabah*	10.50	255
5-year bond	10.25	306	5-year bond	11.00	75
5-year bond	11.00	89	5-year *sukuk mudharabah*	11.00	4
5-year *sukuk mudharabah*	10.25	69			
5-year *sukuk mudharabah*	11.00	5			

IDR = Indonesian rupiah.
Note: *Sukuk mudharabah* are Islamic bonds backed by a profit-sharing scheme from a business venture or partnership.
[a] Multiple issuance of the same tenor indicates issuance on different dates.
Source: Indonesia Stock Exchange.

At the end of December, the 30 largest corporate bond issuers in Indonesia had aggregate outstanding bonds of IDR312.8 trillion, representing 70.2% of the corporate bond total. State-owned energy firm Perusahaan Listrik Negara remained the largest bond issuer, with its bonds outstanding accounting for 6.8% of the corporate total.

Table 3: Top 30 Issuers of Local Currency Corporate Bonds in Indonesia

	Issuers	Outstanding Amount		State-Owned	Listed Company	Type of Industry
		LCY Bonds (IDR billion)	LCY Bonds (USD billion)			
1.	Perusahaan Listrik Negara	30,159	1.94	Yes	No	Energy
2.	Indah Kiat Pulp & Paper	22,260	1.43	No	Yes	Pulp and Paper Manufacturing
3.	Indonesia Eximbank	17,528	1.13	Yes	No	Banking
4.	Bank Rakyat Indonesia	16,759	1.08	Yes	Yes	Banking
5.	Sarana Multi Infrastruktur	16,269	1.05	Yes	No	Finance
6.	Merdeka Copper Gold	13,918	0.89	No	Yes	Mining
7.	Sarana Multigriya Finansial	12,803	0.82	Yes	No	Finance
8.	Pegadaian	12,297	0.79	Yes	No	Finance
9.	Bank Mandiri	11,900	0.76	Yes	Yes	Banking
10.	Wijaya Karya	11,487	0.74	Yes	Yes	Building Construction
11.	Permodalan Nasional Madani	11,028	0.71	Yes	No	Finance
12.	Waskita Karya	9,764	0.63	Yes	Yes	Building Construction
13.	Astra Sedaya Finance	9,600	0.62	No	No	Finance
14.	OKI Pulp & Paper Mills	8,493	0.55	No	No	Pulp and Paper Manufacturing
15.	Chandra Asri Petrochemical	8,380	0.54	No	Yes	Petrochemicals
16.	Tower Bersama Infrastructure	8,208	0.53	No	Yes	Telecommunications Infrastructure Provider
17.	Bank Tabungan Negara	8,182	0.53	Yes	Yes	Banking
18.	Hutama Karya	8,148	0.52	Yes	No	Nonbuilding Construction
19.	Bank Pan Indonesia	7,802	0.50	No	Yes	Banking
20.	Sinar Mas Agro Resources and Technology	7,626	0.49	No	Yes	Food
21.	Indosat	7,596	0.49	No	Yes	Telecommunications
22.	Pupuk Indonesia	7,272	0.47	Yes	No	Chemical Manufacturing
23.	Lontar Papyrus Pulp & Paper Industry	7,050	0.45	No	No	Pulp and Paper Manufacturing
24.	Medco-Energi Internasional	6,795	0.44	No	Yes	Petrochemicals
25.	Bank Pembangunan Daerah Jawa Barat Dan Banten	5,572	0.36	Yes	Yes	Banking
26.	Federal International Finance	5,469	0.35	No	No	Finance
27.	Adira Dinamika Multi Finance	5,447	0.35	No	Yes	Finance
28.	Bank Negara Indonesia	5,000	0.32	Yes	Yes	Banking
29.	Kereta Api Indonesia	5,000	0.32	No	No	Transportation and Logistics
30.	Adhi Karya	4,987	0.32	Yes	Yes	Building Construction
	Total Top 30 LCY Corporate Issuers	312,796	20.09			
	Total LCY Corporate Bonds	445,270	28.60			
	Top 30 as % of Total LCY Corporate Bonds	70.2%	70.2%			

IDR = Indonesian rupiah, LCY = local currency, USD = United States dollar.
Notes:
1. Data as of 31 December 2022.
2. State-owned firms are defined as those in which the government has more than a 50% ownership stake.
Source: *AsianBondsOnline* calculations based on Indonesia Stock Exchange data.

Republic of Korea

The Republic of Korea's local currency (LCY) bond market inched up 0.1% quarter-on-quarter (q-o-q) to KRW2,968.4 trillion (USD2.3 trillion) at the end of December 2022, solely driven by growth in the corporate bond segment. The LCY corporate bond segment posted a marginal increase of 0.4% q-o-q as the growth in corporate bond issuance was capped by maturities; while the size of the LCY government bond market fell 0.3% q-o-q. The outstanding size of central government bonds posted minimal growth of 0.5% q-o-q due to maturities and a decline in issuance following frontloading of issuance in the first half of the year. On a year-on-year basis, the Republic of Korea's LCY bond market expanded 4.5%.

Table 1: Size and Composition of the Local Currency Bond Market in the Republic of Korea

| | Outstanding Amount (billion) | | | | | | Growth Rate (%) | | | |
| | Q4 2021 | | Q3 2022 | | Q4 2022 | | Q4 2021 | | Q4 2022 | |
	KRW	USD	KRW	USD	KRW	USD	q-o-q	y-o-y	q-o-q	y-o-y
Total	2,841,873	2,390	2,964,362	2,071	2,968,401	2,346	1.5	7.9	0.1	4.5
Government	1,182,573	995	1,263,967	883	1,260,504	996	0.2	9.6	(0.3)	6.6
Central Government Bonds	843,660	710	933,074	652	937,507	741	1.4	16.1	0.5	11.1
Central Bank Bonds	140,320	118	123,020	86	112,650	89	(7.1)	(11.9)	(8.4)	(19.7)
Others	198,592	167	207,874	145	210,346	166	0.8	2.9	1.2	5.9
Corporate	1,659,300	1,396	1,700,395	1,188	1,707,897	1,350	2.4	6.8	0.4	2.9

( ) = negative, KRW = Korean won, q-o-q = quarter-on-quarter, Q3 = third quarter, Q4 = fourth quarter, USD = United States dollar, y-o-y = year-on-year.
Notes:
1. Bloomberg LP end-of-period local currency–USD rates are used.
2. Growth rates are calculated from a local currency base and do not include currency effects.
3. "Others" comprise Korea Development Bank bonds, National Housing bonds, and Seoul Metro bonds.
4. Corporate bonds include equity-linked securities and derivatives-linked securities.

Sources: The Bank of Korea and KG Zeroin Corporation.

Issuance of corporate bonds in the Republic of Korea rose 12.4% q-o-q to KRW167.1 trillion in the fourth quarter of 2022 from KRW148.7 trillion in the third quarter. The table below lists some of the notable LCY corporate bond issuances in the Republic of Korea during the quarter.

Table 2: Notable Local Currency Corporate Bond Issuances in the Fourth Quarter of 2022

Corporate Issuers	Coupon Rate (%)	Issued Amount (KRW billion)	Corporate Issuers	Coupon Rate (%)	Issued Amount (KRW billion)
Shinhan Bank[a]			NongHyup Bank[a]		
4-month bond	4.19	310	1-year bond	4.10	440
1-year bond	4.59	490	1-year bond	4.11	200
1-year bond	–	410	Standard Chartered Bank		
1-year bond	4.22	250	1-year bond	4.11	400
Woori Bank[a]			Hyundai Capital Services		
1-year bond	–	280	2-year bond	5.80	310
1-year bond	4.11	250	Hana Bank		
1-year bond	–	230	1-year bond	4.10	300

– = not applicable, KRW = Korean won.
[a] Multiple issuance of the same tenor indicates issuance on different dates.

Source: Based on data from Bloomberg LP.

The top 30 LCY corporate bond issuers in the Republic of Korea comprised 59.4% of total corporate bonds outstanding at the end of December 2022, with an aggregate bond stock of KRW1,015.2 trillion. Korea Housing Finance Corporation, a government-related institution providing financial assistance for social housing, continued to be the largest corporate bond issuer with outstanding bonds of KRW149.3 trillion. Industrial Bank of Korea and Meritz Securities followed with total bonds outstanding of KRW80.9 trillion and KRW74.6 trillion, respectively.

Table 3: Top 30 Issuers of Local Currency Corporate Bonds in the Republic of Korea

	Issuers	Outstanding Amount		State-Owned	Listed on		Type of Industry
		LCY Bonds (KRW billion)	LCY Bonds (USD billion)		KOSPI	KOSDAQ	
1.	Korea Housing Finance Corporation	149,254	117.9	Yes	No	No	Housing Finance
2.	Industrial Bank of Korea	80,930	64.0	Yes	Yes	No	Banking
3.	Meritz Securities	74,644	59.0	No	Yes	No	Securities
4.	Korea Electric Power Corporation	61,190	48.4	Yes	Yes	No	Electricity, Energy, and Power
5.	Hana Securities	49,371	39.0	No	No	No	Securities
6.	Korea Investment and Securities	46,555	36.8	No	No	No	Securities
7.	Shinhan Securities	46,260	36.6	No	No	No	Securities
8.	Mirae Asset Securities	43,996	34.8	No	Yes	No	Securities
9.	KB Securities	40,785	32.2	No	No	No	Securities
10.	Korea Land & Housing Corporation	32,179	25.4	Yes	No	No	Real Estate
11.	NH Investment & Securities	31,123	24.6	No	Yes	No	Securities
12.	The Export-Import Bank of Korea	29,550	23.4	Yes	No	No	Banking
13.	Korea Expressway	27,290	21.6	Yes	No	No	Transport Infrastructure
14.	Shinhan Bank	26,995	21.3	No	No	No	Banking
15.	Samsung Securities	21,906	17.3	No	Yes	No	Securities
16.	Woori Bank	21,550	17.0	No	Yes	No	Banking
17.	Korea SMEs and Startups Agency	21,498	17.0	Yes	No	No	SME Development
18.	KEB Hana Bank	21,331	16.9	No	No	No	Banking
19.	Kookmin Bank	20,594	16.3	No	No	No	Banking
20.	Korea National Railway	19,260	15.2	Yes	No	No	Transport Infrastructure
21.	NongHyup Bank	19,060	15.1	Yes	No	No	Banking
22.	Shinhan Card	17,190	13.6	No	No	No	Credit Card
23.	Hyundai Capital Services	16,710	13.2	No	No	No	Consumer Finance
24.	Shinyoung Securities	15,670	12.4	No	Yes	No	Securities
25.	Hanwha Investment and Securities	14,843	11.7	No	No	No	Securities
26.	KB Kookmin Bank Card	14,585	11.5	No	No	No	Consumer Finance
27.	Standard Chartered Bank Korea	14,210	11.2	No	No	No	Banking
28.	NongHyup	12,940	10.2	Yes	No	No	Banking
29.	Hana Capital	11,920	9.4	No	No	No	Consumer Finance
30.	Korea Railroad Corporation	11,790	9.3	Yes	No	No	Transport Infrastructure
	Total Top 30 LCY Corporate Issuers	1,015,180	802.2				
	Total LCY Corporate Bonds	1,707,897	1,349.6				
	Top 30 as % of Total LCY Corporate Bonds	59.4%	59.4%				

KOSDAQ = Korean Securities Dealer Automated Quotations, KOSPI = Korea Composite Stock Price Index, KRW = Korean won, LCY = local currency, SMEs = small and medium-sized enterprises, USD = United States dollar.
Notes:
1. Data as of 31 December 2022.
2. State-owned firms are defined as those in which the government has more than a 50% ownership stake.
Sources: *AsianBondsOnline* calculations based on Bloomberg LP and KG Zeroin Corporation.

Malaysia

At the end of the fourth quarter (Q4) of 2022, Malaysia's local currency (LCY) bond market reached a size of MYR1,866.9 billion (USD423.9 billion) on growth of 0.8% quarter-on-quarter (q-o-q) and 7.5% year-on-year. Outstanding LCY government bonds inched up marginally by 0.2% q-o-q amid contractions in issuance during the quarter. Outstanding LCY corporate bonds posted growth of 1.4% q-o-q as issuance picked up in Q4 2022, while total outstanding *sukuk* (Islamic bonds) marginally declined 0.1% q-o-q due to maturing securities.

Table 1: Size and Composition of the Local Currency Bond Market in Malaysia

| | Outstanding Amount (billion) | | | | | | Growth Rate (%) | | | |
| | Q4 2021 | | Q3 2022 | | Q4 2022 | | Q4 2021 | | Q4 2022 | |
	MYR	USD	MYR	USD	MYR	USD	q-o-q	y-o-y	q-o-q	y-o-y
Total	1,736	417	1,853	400	1,867	424	1.0	8.2	0.8	7.5
Government	949	228	1,049	226	1,051	239	1.2	11.4	0.2	10.7
Central Government Bonds	931	224	1,035	223	1,041	236	1.9	12.7	0.5	11.8
of which: *sukuk*	441	106	507	109	494	112	1.5	15.0	(2.7)	11.9
Central Bank Bills	0	0	4	0.9	1	0.2	–	(100.0)	(75.9)	–
of which: *sukuk*	0	0	1	0.2	0	0	–	–	(100.0)	–
Sukuk Perumahan Kerajaan	18	4	9	2	9	2	(24.9)	(24.9)	0.0	(49.7)
Corporate	787	189	804	173	816	185	0.8	4.6	1.4	3.7
of which: *sukuk*	643	154	666	144	679	154	0.9	5.7	2.0	5.5

( ) = negative, – = not applicable, MYR = Malaysian ringgit, q-o-q = quarter-on-quarter, Q3 = third quarter, Q4 = fourth quarter, USD = United States dollar, y-o-y = year-on-year.
Notes:
1. Bloomberg LP end-of-period local currency–USD rates are used.
2. Growth rates are calculated from a local currency base and do not include currency effects.
3. *Sukuk* refers to Islamic bonds.
4. Sukuk Perumahan Kerajaan are Islamic bonds issued by the government to refinance funding for housing loans to government employees and to extend new housing loans.
Sources: Bank Negara Malaysia Fully Automated System for Issuing/Tendering and Bloomberg LP.

Issuance of LCY corporate bonds soared 69.7% q-o-q to reach MYR73.2 billion in Q4 2022. Projek Lebuhraya Usahasama Berhad, a subsidiary of toll expressway operator PLUS Malaysia Berhad, had the largest total issuance during the review period.

Table 2: Notable Local Currency Corporate Bond Issuances in the Fourth Quarter of 2022

Corporate Issuers	Coupon Rate (%)	Issued Amount (MYR billion)	Corporate Issuers	Coupon Rate (%)	Issued Amount (MYR billion)
Projek Lebuhraya Usahasama Berhad			Maybank Islamic		
1-year Islamic MTN	4.56	1,000	5-year Islamic MTN	4.33	2,000
2-year Islamic MTN	4.21	160	95-year Islamic MTN	4.76	1,000
13-year Islamic MTN	5.63	1,800	Amanat Lebuhraya Rakyat		
14-year Islamic MTN	5.75	1,800	2-year Islamic MTN	4.28	335
15-year Islamic MTN	5.02	770	8-year Islamic MTN	5.09	460
Cagamas[a]			10-year Islamic MTN	5.24	520
1-year Islamic MTN	3.58	250	11-year Islamic MTN	5.29	485
3-year Islamic MTN	4.27	455	15-year Islamic MTN	5.59	550
5-year MTN	4.55	2,000			
5-year Islamic MTN	4.62	1,000			
5-year MTN	4.71	150			

MTN = medium-term note, MYR = Malaysian ringgit.
[a] Multiple issuance of the same tenor indicates issuance on different dates.
Source: Bank Negara Malaysia Fully Automated System for Issuing/Tendering.

The top 30 corporate bond issuers in Malaysia had a combined total of MYR487.4 billion worth of outstanding LCY bonds at the end of December, representing 59.8% of the LCY corporate bond stock. At the end of 2022, government-owned infrastructure funding company DanaInfra Nasional had the most LCY bonds outstanding, while the finance sector led all sectors in corporate issuance.

Table 3: Top 30 Issuers of Local Currency Corporate Bonds in Malaysia

	Issuers	Outstanding Amount		State-Owned	Listed Company	Type of Industry
		LCY Bonds (MYR billion)	LCY Bonds (USD billion)			
1.	DanaInfra Nasional	82.7	18.8	Yes	No	Finance
2.	Lembaga Pembiayaan Perumahan Sektor Awam	40.3	9.1	Yes	No	Property and Real Estate
3.	Prasarana	39.7	9.0	Yes	No	Transport, Storage, and Communications
4.	Cagamas	37.2	8.4	Yes	No	Finance
5.	Project Lebuhraya Usahasama	36.2	8.2	No	No	Transport, Storage, and Communications
6.	Urusharta Jamaah	27.3	6.2	Yes	No	Finance
7.	Perbadanan Tabung Pendidikan Tinggi Nasional	21.1	4.8	Yes	No	Finance
8.	Pengurusan Air	19.4	4.4	Yes	No	Energy, Gas, and Water
9.	Tenaga Nasional	16.3	3.7	No	Yes	Energy, Gas, and Water
10.	CIMB Group Holdings	14.5	3.3	Yes	No	Finance
11.	Maybank Islamic	13.0	3.0	No	Yes	Banking
12.	Malayan Banking	12.7	2.9	No	Yes	Banking
13.	CIMB Bank	11.6	2.6	Yes	No	Finance
14.	Sarawak Energy	10.8	2.5	Yes	No	Energy, Gas, and Water
15.	Danum Capital	10.1	2.3	No	No	Finance
16.	Danga Capital	10.0	2.3	Yes	No	Finance
17.	Khazanah	9.4	2.1	Yes	No	Finance
18.	Jimah East Power	8.6	1.9	Yes	No	Energy, Gas, and Water
19.	Public Bank	6.9	1.6	No	No	Banking
20.	Malaysia Rail Link	6.8	1.5	Yes	No	Construction
21.	Sapura TMC	6.4	1.4	No	No	Finance
22.	Kuala Lumpur Kepong	5.6	1.3	No	Yes	Energy, Gas, and Water
23.	YTL Power International	5.5	1.3	No	Yes	Energy, Gas, and Water
24.	Amanat Lebuhraya Rakyat	5.5	1.2	No	No	Finance
25.	Bank Pembangunan Malaysia	5.5	1.2	Yes	No	Banking
26.	Bakun Hydro Power Generation	5.1	1.2	No	No	Energy, Gas, and Water
27.	1Malaysia Development	5.0	1.1	Yes	No	Finance
28.	EDRA Energy	4.9	1.1	No	Yes	Energy, Gas, and Water
29.	Infracap Resources	4.9	1.1	Yes	No	Finance
30.	PNB Merdeka Ventures	4.8	1.1	No	No	Finance
Total Top 30 LCY Corporate Issuers		**487.4**	**110.7**			
Total LCY Corporate Bonds		**815.8**	**185.2**			
Top 30 as % of Total LCY Corporate Bonds		**59.8%**	**59.8%**			

LCY = local currency, MYR = Malaysian ringgit, USD = United States dollar.
Notes:
1. Data as of 31 December 2022.
2. State-owned firms are defined as those in which the government has more than a 50% ownership stake.
Source: *AsianBondsOnline* calculations based on Bank Negara Malaysia Fully Automated System for Issuing/Tendering data.

Philippines

The local currency (LCY) bond market of the Philippines grew a marginal 0.2% quarter-on-quarter (q-o-q) in the fourth quarter (Q4) of 2022 to reach a size of PHP11,196.5 billion (USD200.9 billion) at the end of December. Outstanding government bonds declined, driven by maturities exceeding the issuance of Treasury bills and other government securities. The outstanding stock of corporate bonds grew 4.4% q-o-q amid increased issuance volume during the quarter. At the end of December, the Philippines' LCY bond market comprised 85.7% government bonds and 14.3% corporate bonds.

Table 1: Size and Composition of the Local Currency Bond Market in the Philippines

| | Outstanding Amount (billion) | | | | | | Growth Rate (%) | | | |
| | Q4 2021 | | Q3 2022 | | Q4 2022 | | Q4 2021 | | Q4 2022 | |
	PHP	USD	PHP	USD	PHP	USD	q-o-q	y-o-y	q-o-q	y-o-y
Total	9,880	194	11,17	190	11,196	201	0.5	14.8	0.2	13.3
Government	8,365	164	9,636	164	9,593	172	0.5	20.3	(0.4)	14.7
Treasury Bills	796	16	509	9	410	7	(15.5)	(16.1)	(19.4)	(48.5)
Treasury Bonds	7,267	143	8,669	148	8,681	156	5.6	27.0	0.1	19.5
Central Bank Securities	260	5	410	7	480	9	(40.9)	18.2	17.1	84.6
Others	42	0.8	48	0.8	22	0.4	(30.3)	(36.6)	(54.2)	(47.3)
Corporate	1,515	30	1,535	26	1,603	29	0.6	(8.1)	4.4	5.8

( ) = negative, PHP = Philippine peso, q-o-q = quarter-on-quarter, Q3 = third quarter, Q4 = fourth quarter, USD = United States dollar, y-o-y = year-on-year.
Notes:
1. Bloomberg end-of-period local currency–USD rates are used.
2. Growth rates are calculated from a local currency base and do not include currency effects.
3. "Others" comprise bonds issued by government agencies, entities, and corporations for which repayment is guaranteed by the Government of the Philippines. This includes bonds issued by Power Sector Assets and Liabilities Management (PSALM) and the National Food Authority, among others.
4. Peso Global Bonds (PHP-denominated bonds payable in US dollars) are not included.
Sources: Bloomberg LP and Bureau of the Treasury.

Higher borrowing costs capped corporate bond issuance as growth decelerated to 1.6% q-o-q in Q4 2022 from 37.7% q-o-q in the third quarter. Total issuance climbed to PHP127.5 billion from PHP125.5 billion in the previous quarter. In Q4 2022, 16 LCY corporate bonds were issued by eight companies. San Miguel was the top issuer during the period with PHP60.0 billion worth of multitranche bond issuances.

Table 2: Notable Local Currency Corporate Bond Issuances in the Fourth Quarter of 2022

Corporate Issuers	Coupon Rate (%)	Issued Amount (PHP billion)	Corporate Issuers	Coupon Rate (%)	Issued Amount (PHP billion)
San Miguel			Security Bank		
5.3-year bond	7.45	27.10	1.5-year bond	5.30	14.60
7-year bond	7.85	9.71	Cebu Landmasters		
10-year bond	8.49	23.19	3.5-year bond	6.42	2.77
Metropolitan Bank			5.5-year bond	6.99	1.24
1.5-year bond	5.00	23.72	7-year bond	7.36	0.99
Aboitiz Equity Ventures					
3.5-year bond	6.87	9.10			
7-year bond	7.53	10.90			

PHP = Philippine peso.
Source: Based on data from Bloomberg LP.

At the end of December, the Philippines' top 30 corporate issuers had aggregate LCY bonds outstanding of PHP1,453.0 billion, accounting for 90.6% of the total LCY corporate bond market. The banking sector continued to hold the largest market share at 32.8%, followed by property firms at 28.7% and holding firms at 22.4%. San Miguel, Ayala Land, and SM Prime Holdings were the top three issuers of LCY corporate bonds, representing 10.2%, 9.3%, and 7.5%, respectively, of the total corporate bond market at the end of December.

Table 3: Top 30 Issuers of Local Currency Corporate Bonds in the Philippines

	Issuers	Outstanding Amount		State-Owned	Listed Company	Type of Industry
		LCY Bonds (PHP billion)	LCY Bonds (USD billion)			
1.	San Miguel	163.3	2.9	No	Yes	Holding Firms
2.	Ayala Land	149.3	2.7	No	Yes	Property
3.	SM Prime Holdings	119.6	2.1	No	Yes	Property
4.	Metropolitan Bank	100.0	1.8	No	Yes	Banking
5.	BDO Unibank	96.5	1.7	No	Yes	Banking
6.	SMC Global Power	90.1	1.6	No	No	Electricity, Energy, and Power
7.	Security Bank	65.4	1.2	No	Yes	Banking
8.	Ayala Corporation	55.0	1.0	No	Yes	Holding Firms
9.	Aboitiz Power	54.4	1.0	No	Yes	Electricity, Energy, and Power
10.	Rizal Commercial Banking Corporation	48.7	0.9	No	Yes	Banking
11.	SM Investments	48.3	0.9	No	Yes	Holding Firms
12.	Aboitiz Equity Ventures	47.6	0.9	No	Yes	Holding Firms
13.	Petron	45.0	0.8	No	Yes	Electricity, Energy, and Power
14.	Vista Land	42.6	0.8	No	Yes	Property
15.	Bank of the Philippine Islands	42.4	0.8	No	Yes	Banking
16.	Union Bank of the Philippines	37.0	0.7	No	Yes	Banking
17.	Filinvest Land	35.4	0.6	No	Yes	Property
18.	China Bank	30.3	0.5	No	Yes	Banking
19.	Robinsons Land	29.6	0.5	No	Yes	Property
20.	Philippine National Bank	19.2	0.3	No	Yes	Banking
21.	Maynilad	18.5	0.3	No	No	Water
22.	Doubledragon	15.0	0.3	No	Yes	Property
23.	San Miguel Food and Beverage	15.0	0.3	No	Yes	Food and Beverages
24.	Cebu Landmasters	13.0	0.2	No	Yes	Property
25.	Philippine Savings Bank	12.7	0.2	No	Yes	Banking
26.	Bank of Commerce	12.5	0.2	No	Yes	Banking
27.	Megaworld	12.0	0.2	No	Yes	Property
28.	Puregold	12.0	0.2	No	Yes	Whole and Retail Trading
29.	Metro Pacific Investments	11.4	0.2	No	Yes	Holding Firms
30.	East West Banking	11.2	0.2	No	Yes	Banking
	Total Top 30 LCY Corporate Issuers	**1,453.0**	**26.1**			
	Total LCY Corporate Bonds	**1,603.1**	**28.8**			
	Top 30 as % of Total LCY Corporate Bonds	**90.6%**	**90.6%**			

LCY = local currency, PHP = Philippine peso, USD = United States dollar.
Notes:
1. Data as of 31 December 2022.
2. State-owned firms are defined as those in which the government has more than a 50% ownership stake.
Source: *AsianBondsOnline* calculations based on Bloomberg LP data.

Singapore

In the fourth quarter (Q4) of 2022, Singapore's local currency (LCY) bond market expanded 2.4% quarter-on-quarter (q-o-q) and 12.8% year-on-year, reaching a size of SGD661.8 billion (USD494.0 billion) at the end of December. Outstanding LCY government bonds jumped 2.9% q-o-q and LCY corporate bonds grew 1.2% q-o-q on declining maturities during the quarter.

Table 1: Size and Composition of the Local Currency Bond Market in Singapore

| | Outstanding Amount (billion) | | | | | | Growth Rate (%) | | | |
| | Q4 2021 | | Q3 2022 | | Q4 2022 | | Q4 2021 | | Q4 2022 | |
	SGD	USD	SGD	USD	SGD	USD	q-o-q	y-o-y	q-o-q	y-o-y
Total	586	435	646	450	662	494	3.2	17.9	2.4	12.8
Government	412	305	469	327	482	360	4.1	24.9	2.9	17.2
SGS Bills and Bonds	214	159	230	160	234	174	(0.6)	9.2	1.8	9.1
MAS Bills	197	146	240	167	249	186	9.7	48.0	3.8	26.1
Corporate	175	130	177	124	179	134	1.0	4.2	1.2	2.5

( ) = negative, MAS = Monetary Authority of Singapore, q-o-q = quarter-on-quarter, Q3 = third quarter, Q4 = fourth quarter, SGD = Singapore dollar, SGS = Singapore Government Securities, USD = United States dollar, y-o-y = year-on-year.
Notes:
1. Corporate bonds are based on *AsianBondsOnline* estimates.
2. SGS bills and bonds do not include the special issue of SGS held by the Singapore Central Provident Fund.
3. Bloomberg LP end-of-period local currency–USD rates are used.
4. Growth rates are calculated from a local currency base and do not include currency effects.

Sources: Bloomberg LP and Monetary Authority of Singapore.

During the quarter, issuance of LCY corporate bonds decreased 31.9% q-o-q to SGD2.6 billion as interest rates remained high due to monetary policy tightening by the central bank. The government-owned Housing & Development Board had the most total issuance in Q4 2022.

Table 2: Notable Local Currency Corporate Bond Issuances in the Fourth Quarter of 2022

Corporate Issuers	Coupon Rate (%)	Issued Amount (SGD million)
Housing & Development Board		
5-year bond	4.090	1,200.0
7-year bond	3.995	900.0
Centurion Corporation		
3-year bond	6.500	53.0
Koh Brothers		
3-year bond	6.500	22.8
Addvalue Technologies		
5-year bond	6.000	5.0

SGD = Singapore dollar.
Source: Bloomberg LP.

At the end of 2022, the top 30 corporate bond issuers had a total of SGD109.8 billion worth of outstanding LCY corporate bonds, equivalent to 61.2% of the LCY corporate bond market of Singapore. In terms of outstanding corporate bonds at the end of Q4 2022, the Housing & Development Board continued to top all issuers, with the real estate sector topping all sectors.

Table 3: Top 30 Issuers of Local Currency Corporate Bonds in Singapore

	Issuers	Outstanding Amount		State-Owned	Listed Company	Type of Industry
		LCY Bonds (SGD billion)	LCY Bonds (USD billion)			
1.	Housing & Development Board	30.1	22.5	Yes	No	Real Estate
2.	Singapore Airlines	14.7	11.0	Yes	Yes	Transportation
3.	Land Transport Authority	8.9	6.6	Yes	No	Transportation
4.	Temasek Financial	5.1	3.8	Yes	No	Finance
5.	CapitaLand	4.6	3.4	Yes	Yes	Real Estate
6.	United Overseas Bank	4.4	3.3	No	Yes	Banking
7.	Sembcorp Industries	4.1	3.1	No	Yes	Diversified
8.	Frasers Property	3.8	2.9	No	Yes	Real Estate
9.	Mapletree Treasury Services	3.3	2.4	No	No	Finance
10.	DBS Bank	2.9	2.1	No	Yes	Banking
11.	Oversea-Chinese Banking Corporation	2.2	1.6	No	Yes	Banking
12.	Keppel Corporation	2.2	1.6	No	Yes	Diversified
13.	CapitaLand Mall Trust	2.0	1.5	No	No	Finance
14.	City Developments Limited	2.0	1.5	No	Yes	Real Estate
15.	Public Utilities Board	1.7	1.3	Yes	No	Utilities
16.	Singapore Technologies Telemedia	1.7	1.3	Yes	No	Utilities
17.	National Environment Agency	1.7	1.2	Yes	No	Environmental Services
18.	Shangri-La Hotel	1.5	1.1	No	Yes	Real Estate
19.	Suntec Real Estate Investment Trust	1.4	1.1	No	Yes	Real Estate
20.	Ascendas Real Estate Investment Trust	1.3	1.0	No	Yes	Finance
21.	PSA Treasury	1.3	1.0	Yes	No	Transportation
22.	Singtel Group Treasury	1.3	0.9	No	No	Finance
23.	Ascott Residence	1.1	0.8	No	Yes	Real Estate
24.	GuocoLand Limited IHT	1.1	0.8	No	No	Real Estate
25.	Keppel Infrastructure Trust	1.1	0.8	No	No	Diversified
26.	Olam Group	1.0	0.7	No	Yes	Consumer Goods
27.	Singapore Post	1.0	0.7	No	Yes	Transportation
28.	Singapore Press Holdings	1.0	0.7	No	Yes	Communications
29.	Hyflux	0.9	0.7	No	Yes	Utilities
30.	Mapletree Logistics Trust	0.9	0.7	No	Yes	Real Estate
	Total Top 30 LCY Corporate Issuers	109.8	82.0			
	Total LCY Corporate Bonds	179.4	133.9			
	Top 30 as % of Total LCY Corporate Bonds	61.2%	61.2%			

LCY = local currency, SGD = Singapore dollar, USD = United States dollar.
Notes:
1. Data as of 31 December 2022.
2. State-owned firms are defined as those in which the government has more than a 50% ownership stake.
Source: *AsianBondsOnline* calculations based on Bloomberg LP data.

Thailand

The local currency (LCY) bond market in Thailand reached a size of THB15.6 trillion (USD451.5 billion) at the end of the fourth quarter (Q4) of 2022. Overall growth slowed to 0.8% quarter-on-quarter (q-o-q) in Q4 2022 from 2.6% q-o-q the third quarter, as the government started to roll back its pandemic-related borrowing in the new fiscal year starting in October, while higher interest rates capped corporate issuance. The Government of Thailand issued THB30.0 billion of sustainability bonds in December. Annual growth in Thailand's LCY bond market inched down to 6.1% in Q4 2022 from 6.4% in the prior quarter.

Table 1: Size and Composition of the Local Currency Bond Market in Thailand

| | Outstanding Amount (billion) | | | | | | Growth Rate (%) | | | |
| | Q4 2021 | | Q3 2022 | | Q4 2022 | | Q4 2021 | | Q4 2022 | |
	THB	USD	THB	USD	THB	USD	q-o-q	y-o-y	q-o-q	y-o-y
Total	14,728	441	15,496	411	15,625	452	1.1	5.8	0.8	6.1
Government	10,716	321	11,105	294	11,171	323	1.6	4.7	0.6	4.2
Government Bonds and Treasury Bills	6,883	206	7,603	201	7,771	225	3.0	14.3	2.2	12.9
Central Bank Bonds	2,898	87	2,522	67	2,403	69	(1.0)	(13.9)	(4.7)	(17.1)
State-Owned Enterprise and Other Bonds	936	28	980	26	997	29	(0.7)	10.6	1.7	6.6
Corporate	4,011	120	4,392	116	4,454	129	0.01	8.6	1.4	11.0

( ) = negative, q-o-q = quarter-on-quarter, Q3 = third quarter, Q4 = fourth quarter, THB = Thai baht, USD = United States dollar, y-o-y = year-on-year.
Notes:
1. Bloomberg end-of-period local currency–USD rates are used.
2. Growth rates are calculated from a local currency base and do not include currency effects.
Source: Bank of Thailand.

New issuance of LCY corporate bonds amounted to THB496.3 billion in Q4 2022, down from THB556.8 billion in the preceding quarter. Issuance continued to contract, declining 10.9% q-o-q in Q4 2022 after falling 6.9% q-o-q in the third quarter amid rising borrowing costs as the Bank of Thailand continued its gradual monetary policy tightening to combat inflation. The largest issuer during the quarter was Ek-Chai Distribution System, a retail company, which raised a total of THB23.5 billion from a quadruple-tranche bond issuance.

Table 2: Notable Local Currency Corporate Bond Issuances in the Fourth Quarter of 2022

Corporate Issuers	Coupon Rate (%)	Issued Amount (THB billion)	Corporate Issuers	Coupon Rate (%)	Issued Amount (THB billion)
Ek-Chai Distribution System			True Corporation		
1.5-year bond	2.81	9.8	2-year bond	3.50	4.2
3-year bond	3.25	8.5	4-year bond	4.35	2.1
5-year bond	3.55	1.2	5-year bond	4.90	3.1
7-year bond	4.00	3.9	5.8-year bond	5.05	6.5
Bank of Ayudhya			Siam Cement		
10-year bond	4.30	16.5	4-year bond	3.25	15.0
BTS Group[a]					
2-year bond	2.95	4.1			
2-year bond	2.95	1.6			
4.5-year bond	3.85	5.0			
4.5-year bond	3.85	1.9			
7.5-year bond	4.35	1.9			
10-year bond	4.70	1.6			

THB = Thai baht.
[a] Multiple issuance of the same tenor indicates issuance on different dates.
Source: Bloomberg LP.

The outstanding bonds of the top 30 nonbank corporate issuers in Thailand reached THB2,527.4 billion at the end of December, accounting for a 56.7% share of the LCY corporate bond market. CP ALL, True Corporation, and PTT remained the top issuers with outstanding bond stocks representing 5.3%, 4.2%, and 3.6%, respectively, of the Thai corporate bond market. Energy and utilities firms accounted for the most outstanding corporate bonds among all sectors, amounting to a combined THB482.9 billion.

Table 3: Top 30 Issuers of Local Currency Corporate Bonds in Thailand

	Issuers	LCY Bonds (THB billion)	LCY Bonds (USD billion)	State-Owned	Listed Company	Type of Industry
1.	CP ALL	234.1	6.8	No	Yes	Commerce
2.	True Corporation	185.4	5.4	No	Yes	Communications
3.	PTT	158.4	4.6	Yes	Yes	Energy and Utilities
4.	Thai Beverage	142.2	4.1	No	No	Food and Beverage
5.	Siam Cement	140.0	4.0	Yes	Yes	Construction Materials
6.	Charoen Pokphand Foods	131.5	3.8	No	Yes	Food and Beverage
7.	Berli Jucker	107.4	3.1	No	Yes	Commerce
8.	Gulf Energy Development	104.5	3.0	No	Yes	Energy and Utilities
9.	True Move H Universal Communication	98.6	2.8	No	No	Communications
10.	CPF Thailand	89.2	2.6	No	No	Food and Beverage
11.	PTT Global Chemical	86.7	2.5	No	Yes	Petrochemicals and Chemicals
12.	Indorama Ventures	78.4	2.3	No	Yes	Petrochemicals and Chemicals
13.	Banpu	78.4	2.3	No	Yes	Energy and Utilities
14.	Bangkok Commercial Asset Management	73.1	2.1	No	Yes	Finance and Securities
15.	BTS Group Holdings	72.8	2.1	No	Yes	Transportation and Logistics
16.	Bank of Ayudhya	64.9	1.9	No	Yes	Banking
17.	Minor International	62.4	1.8	No	Yes	Hospitality and Leisure
18.	Muangthai Capital	59.9	1.7	No	Yes	Finance and Securities
19.	Toyota Leasing Thailand	55.0	1.6	No	No	Finance and Securities
20.	Global Power Synergy	51.5	1.5	No	Yes	Energy and Utilities
21.	dtac TriNet	50.4	1.5	No	Yes	Communications
22.	TPI Polene	50.3	1.5	No	Yes	Construction Materials
23.	Bangchak	49.5	1.4	No	Yes	Energy and Utilities
24.	Magnolia Quality Development	48.6	1.4	No	No	Property Development
25.	Krungthai Card	45.7	1.3	No	Yes	Finance and Securities
26.	Sansiri	45.4	1.3	No	Yes	Property Development
27.	Krung Thai Bank	42.1	1.2	Yes	Yes	Banking
28.	Bangkok Expressway & Metro	41.6	1.2	No	Yes	Transportation and Logistics
29.	B Grimm Power	40.7	1.2	No	Yes	Energy and Utilities
30.	Kiatnakin Phatra Bank	39.1	1.1	No	Yes	Banking
	Total Top 30 LCY Corporate Issuers	2,527.4	73.0			
	Total LCY Corporate Bonds	4,454.0	128.7			
	Top 30 as % of Total LCY Corporate Bonds	56.7%	56.7%			

LCY = local currency, THB = Thai baht, USD = United States dollar.
Notes:
1. Data as of 31 December 2022.
2. State-owned firms are defined as those in which the government has more than a 50% ownership stake.
Source: *AsianBondsOnline* calculations based on Bloomberg LP data.

Viet Nam

In the fourth quarter (Q4) of 2022, growth in the local currency (LCY) bond market of Viet Nam accelerated to 6.5% quarter-on-quarter (q-o-q), with the outstanding bond stock reaching VND2,498.5 trillion (USD105.7 billion). The higher growth was mainly driven by government bonds amid increased issuance of Treasury bonds and government-guaranteed bonds during the quarter. In contrast, the corporate bond stock contracted due to continued bond repurchases by issuers and a decline in issuance volume on tighter corporate bond regulations.

Table 1: Size and Composition of the Local Currency Bond Market in Viet Nam

| | Outstanding Amount (billion) | | | | | | Growth Rate (%) | | | |
| | Q4 2021 | | Q3 2022 | | Q4 2022 | | Q4 2021 | | Q4 2022 | |
	VND	USD	VND	USD	VND	USD	q-o-q	y-o-y	q-o-q	y-o-y
Total	2,089,053	92	2,345,688	98	2,498,515	106	8.8	25.5	6.5	19.6
Government	1,489,606	65	1,608,839	67	1,768,424	75	4.3	8.0	9.9	18.7
Treasury Bonds	1,349,811	59	1,435,693	60	1,525,134	65	5.1	9.9	6.2	13.0
Central Bank Bills	0	0	30,400	1	94,400	4	–	–	210.5	–
Government Guaranteed and Municipal Bonds	139,796	6	142,747	6	148,890	6	(2.3)	(7.6)	4.3	6.5
Corporate	599,446	26	736,850	31	730,092	31	21.9	110.0	(0.9)	21.8

( ) = negative, – = not applicable, q-o-q = quarter-on-quarter, Q3 = third quarter, Q4 = fourth quarter, USD = United States dollar, VND = Vietnamese dong, y-o-y = year-on-year.
Notes:
1. Bloomberg LP end-of-period local currency–USD rates are used.
2. Growth rates are calculated from a local currency base and do not include currency effects.
Sources: Bloomberg LP and Vietnam Bond Market Association.

Viet Nam's corporate bond issuance in Q4 2022 substantially dropped 92.3% q-o-q to VND3,844.7 trillion. There were only 17 corporate bond issuances during the quarter, all of which were privately placed and issued by a total of 10 companies. Since most corporate bonds in Viet Nam are issued via private placement, the enforcement of Decree 65 in September dragged down overall issuance during the quarter.[12]

Table 2: Notable Local Currency Corporate Bond Issuances in the Fourth Quarter of 2022

Corporate Issuer	Coupon Rate (%)	Issued Amount (VND billion)
Masan Group		
5-year bond	4.10% + average interest rate for 12-month deposit	1,700
Nam Long Investment		
7-year bond	3.50% + fixed base rate	500
Thanh Nguyen Energy Development and Investment		
5-year bond	13.00% (first year)	500

Corporate Issuer	Coupon Rate (%)	Issued Amount (VND billion)
Bank for Investment and Development of Vietnam		
6-year bond	1.30% + average interest rate for 12-month deposit	45
7-year bond	1.35% + average interest rate for 12-month deposit	40
20-year bond	8.50%	200
Nui Phao Mining		
5-year bond	11.00% (first 2 years)	210

VND = Vietnamese dong.
Source: Vietnam Bond Market Association.

[12] Decree 65 establishes tighter regulatory restrictions in the issuance process, including bond registration and use of bond proceeds, of privately placed corporate bonds. Issuers are subjected to tighter disclosure requirements, and the refinancing of privately placed bonds is restricted to issuers themselves and not for their subsidiaries or affiliated companies. Decree 65 also specifies that bond proceeds can no longer be used to finance or restructure the issuers' capital resources and requires bond issuers to redeem the bond ahead of maturity if they violate the regulations on bond issuance and trading, or if they breach the bond issuance plan.

In Q4 2022, the aggregate LCY bonds outstanding of the top 30 corporate issuers reached VND469.3 trillion, accounting for 64.3% of the total LCY corporate bond market. Majority of the top 30 corporate issuers were from the banking sector, having a total debt stock equivalent to 80.9% of the outstanding total of the top 30 issuers. The property sector had the second-largest share at 10.7%, amounting to VND50.4 trillion.

Table 3: Top 30 Issuers of Local Currency Corporate Bonds in Viet Nam

	Issuers	Outstanding Amount		State-Owned	Listed Company	Type of Industry
		LCY Bonds (VND billion)	LCY Bonds (USD billion)			
1.	Bank for Investment and Development of Vietnam	61,115	2.59	Yes	Yes	Banking
2.	Vietnam Prosperity Joint Stock Commercial Bank	30,600	1.29	No	Yes	Banking
3.	Orient Commercial Joint Stock Bank	29,535	1.25	No	No	Banking
4.	Ho Chi Minh City Development Joint Stock Commercial Bank	29,182	1.23	No	Yes	Banking
5.	Vietnam International Joint Stock Commercial Bank	28,950	1.22	No	Yes	Banking
6.	Lien Viet Post Joint Stock Commercial Bank	28,344	1.20	No	Yes	Banking
7.	Asia Commercial Joint Stock Bank	27,700	1.17	No	Yes	Banking
8.	Vietnam Joint Stock Commercial Bank for Industry and Trade	25,102	1.06	Yes	Yes	Banking
9.	Masan Group	21,200	0.90	No	Yes	Diversified
10.	Military Commercial Joint Stock Bank	18,846	0.80	No	Yes	Banking
11.	Tien Phong Commercial Joint Stock Bank	17,949	0.76	No	Yes	Banking
12.	Vietnam Technological and Commercial Joint Stock Bank	14,300	0.61	No	Yes	Banking
13.	NoVa Real Estate Investment Corporation JSC	12,281	0.52	No	Yes	Property
14.	An Binh Commercial Joint Stock Bank	11,300	0.48	No	No	Banking
15.	Saigon—Ha Noi Commercial Joint Stock Bank	10,150	0.43	No	Yes	Banking
16.	Vinhomes JSC	9,935	0.42	No	Yes	Property
17.	Vietnam Maritime Joint Stock Commercial Bank	9,399	0.40	No	Yes	Banking
18.	Vietnam Bank for Agriculture and Rural Development	8,657	0.37	Yes	No	Banking
19.	Sovico Group Joint Stock Company	8,550	0.36	No	Yes	Consumer Services
20.	Bank for Foreign Trade of Vietnam JSC	8,240	0.35	No	No	Banking
21.	Saigon Glory Company Limited	8,000	0.34	No	No	Property
22.	Southeast Asia Commercial Joint Stock Bank	7,826	0.33	No	Yes	Banking
23.	Bac A Commercial Joint Stock Bank	7,535	0.32	No	Yes	Banking
24.	Golden Hill Real Estate JSC	5,701	0.24	No	No	Property
25.	Vingroup	5,425	0.23	No	Yes	Property
26.	Ho Chi Minh City Infrastructure Investment	5,113	0.22	No	Yes	Construction
27.	Sai Gon Thuong Tin Commercial Joint Stock Bank	4,800	0.20	No	Yes	Banking
28.	Thai Son—Long An JSC	4,600	0.19	No	No	Property
29.	VPBank SMBC Finance Company Limited	4,500	0.19	No	No	Finance
30.	Phu My Hung Corporation	4,497	0.19	No	No	Property
	Total Top 30 LCY Corporate Issuers	469,330	19.86			
	Total LCY Corporate Bonds	730,092	30.89			
	Top 30 as % of Total LCY Corporate Bonds	64.3%	64.3%			

LCY = local currency, USD = United States dollar, VND = Vietnamese dong.
Notes:
1. Data as of 31 December 2022.
2. State-owned firms are defined as those in which the government has more than a 50% ownership stake.
Source: *AsianBondsOnline* calculations based on Bloomberg LP and Vietnam Bond Market Association data.